RECORDS

OF

THE FIRST BATTALION
THE ROYAL DUBLIN FUSILIERS

FIELD-MARSHAL H.R.H.
ARTHUR WILLIAM PATRICK ALBERT, DUKE OF CONNAUGHT AND STRATHEARN.
K.G., K.T., K.P., G.C.B., etc.
Colonel-In-Chief The Royal Dublin Fusiliers.

THE

REGIMENTAL RECORDS

OF

THE FIRST BATTALION
THE ROYAL DUBLIN FUSILIERS

FORMERLY

THE MADRAS EUROPEANS

THE MADRAS EUROPEAN REGIMENT

THE FIRST MADRAS FUSILIERS

THE 102ND ROYAL MADRAS FUSILIERS

1644-1842

BY ONE WHOSE WHOLE SERVICE WAS PASSED IN THE CORPS

AND WHO HAD THE HONOUR OF COMMANDING IT

LONDON

HUGH REES, Ltd.

119 PALL MALL, S.W.

1910

THE ARMS, COLOURS, ACCOUTREMENTS AND TROPHIES
OF THE REGIMENT.

PREFACE

THE history of the Madras European Regiment, now the 1st Battalion the Royal Dublin Fusiliers, from its inception in 1644 to the year 1842, was most ably written by the late General Neill of the regiment from official records, the journals of General Stringer Lawrence, its first Colonel, from Ormes' 'History of India,' and other reliable sources; but the work in question, consisting as it does of but one chapter containing no less than 575 pages, with the leaves undated, and containing much unnecessary detail, it has occurred to the writer and to many others, that without any departure from its historical facts the time has arrived for a more modern and less prolix rendering; consequently, the new volume is written with the sole object of so arranging the chapters and dates that the services of the battalion, extending over a period of nearly two centuries, may be presented in a clear and readable form.

In fighting the battles of their native land, the Royal Dublin Fusiliers, under that and former designations, have ever been famous for their valour and fortitude, having borne a distinguished part in almost every service in Asia and Africa, where British troops have been engaged.

The services of the regiment are therefore placed on record in order that the inheritors of its fame may for all time bear in grateful memory its gallant exploits, which in so large a degree have conduced to the civilisation, peace, and security of millions of His Imperial Majesty's subjects.

The names of Stringer Lawrence, Clive, Dalton, Caillaud, Joseph Smith, Malcolm, Munro, and many others are well known to history, but there still remains a long list of heroes, both amongst officers and men, whose actions were as noble and whose endurance was as great, though their valorous deeds have not been so prominently recorded.

The history of the corps between the years 1644 and 1842 is the history of the British Empire in India during that period, and to the officers and men of the regiment a record of its deeds cannot but prove highly interesting and instructive, containing as it does the services of one of the oldest corps in the British Army, and one in which so many illustrious and great characters belonging to it have taken part.

G. J. HARCOURT.

CAMBERLEY, SURREY.
October 1909.

CONTENTS

CHAPTER VI

(1752 to 1753)

CHAPTER VII

(1753)

CHAPTER VIII

(1753 to 1755)

CHAPTER IX

(1755 to 1757)

CHAPTER X

(1757 to 1759)

CONTENTS

ILLUSTRATIONS

RECORDS

OF THE

FIRST BATTALION THE ROYAL DUBLIN FUSILIERS

CHAPTER I

IN the month of March 1644 thirty recruits landed at Fort St. George, Madras, from England, and in the following year twenty more arrived; these formed the nucleus of a body of men subsequently divided into seven independent companies of 100 men each, commanded by ensigns, and known until the year 1748 as the 'Madras Europeans.'

1644

In addition to garrisoning the different factories on the Coromandel coast, detachments of the corps were sent from Fort St. George to the factories at Bantam, Java, Priaman, and Formosa. These factories were either fortifications, or structures sufficiently strong to afford protection from the dangers constantly threatened by the rapacity of the native princes in whose territories they were situated.

1648

In 1653 Fort St. George was raised to the rank of a Presidency; and from the earliest times the troops of the East India Company were armed, disciplined, clothed, and accoutred after the fashion of the Royal Army.

1653

1665   In 1665 a company consisted of 100 men, sixty of whom were armed with muskets, ten with light firelocks, and thirty with long pikes who formed in the centre on each side of the colours ; each soldier carried a sword, and those with firearms a dagger, the handle of which was made to fit, when required, into the muzzle of the musket.

1676   In 1676 the soldiers' pay was fixed at the rate of £1 1s. *per mensem* in full, for provisions and necessaries of every description.

1677   During the year 1677 the great Mahratta General Sivajee threatened Madras, but retired after taking Gingee and Nellore from the Nawab of the Carnatic, leaving the bulk of his army behind with strict orders to surprise and plunder Madras on the first favourable opportunity.   At the same time the seaport of Pondicherry, seventy-five miles south of Madras, was consigned to the French by Aurungzebe, the Emperor of Delhi.

1682   In 1682, European interlopers having threatened the agent of the English factory at Hoogly near Calcutta, an ensign of tried courage and thirty soldiers of the corps were sent from Fort St. George for his protection, and were the first British soldiers sent to Bengal.

1686   In 1686 bayonets were introduced.   The captains carried a pike, the lieutenants partisans, the ensigns half-pikes, and the serjeants halberds ; all in addition wore swords.

In this year, also, England declared war against the Nawab of Dacca, in Bengal ; a fleet of ten ships was dispatched under Captain Nicholson, and was joined by a detachment of the Madras Europeans from Madras, as, also, a company of the corps from Priaman, situated on the island of Sumatra, which place was garrisoned by 300 men of the corps, and mounted forty-nine guns.

FORT ST. GEORGE, MADRAS.

(*From a painting by George Lambert and Samuel Scott, now in the India Office.*)

A severe action ensued at Hoogly, in which the Nawab's troops were defeated, sixty being killed and many wounded ; a battery of eleven guns was carried by the British, and the town was bombarded and destroyed.

This was the first action fought by the British in Bengal. The English settlement was then moved towards what is now Calcutta, where shortly afterwards it was again attacked by the Nawab; the chief, Mr. Job Charnock, making a gallant defence, repulsing the repeated assaults of the Nawab's troops, and eventually storming and capturing their forts at Tanna and Injellee.

1688
1689
During 1688–89 the factory of Vizagapatam in the Northern Circars, garrisoned by a detachment of the corps, was surprised by one of the Emperor Aurungzebe's armies, every person belonging to it being killed. In 1689, also, Fort St. David, ninety miles south of Madras, was established.

1703
1704
During 1703–4 Madras was besieged by the Mahomedans, but they were repulsed by the garrison.

In 1703 pikes were abolished, and every soldier was armed with a musket, bayonet, and sword ; the officers and non-commissioned officers in addition to their swords carried, the former spontoons, the latter halberds.

The ammunition was carried in a leather pouch suspended by a broad buff belt over the left shoulder, and hanging over the left hip ; the bayonet and sword were attached on the left side to a broad buff waist belt.

1741
In June 1741 a large Mahratta army besieged Fort St. George, but after a short investment they withdrew. In December, however, they returned, but were driven back.

1745
In 1745 war was declared between England and France. In July an English squadron of four

small ships under Commodore Barnet appeared on the Coromandel Coast and landed a few recruits at Fort St. George. The garrison of Pondicherry at this time amounted to 436 French soldiers, that of the English at Forts St. George and St. David to about 150 men each.

1746 In August 1746, the French army having increased to nearly 3,000 men, the Marquis Dupleix, the French Governor-General, resolved, in the absence of the British fleet, to lay siege to Fort St. George, and to accomplish this he dispatched M. Labourdonais from Pondicherry by sea with 1,100 French soldiers, 400 Caffirs, 400 sepoys, and 2,000 French seamen.

The bombardment was kept up for three days, from the 7th to the 10th of September, when the fort being untenable surrendered, with a loss to the detachment of the corps in garrison, consisting of about 200 men, of seven killed and wounded, and Madras was given up, after having been in the possession of the British for upwards of one hundred years. The Company's troops were made prisoners of war, but the majority of the officers and several of the men contrived to make their escape to Fort St. David, which on the surrender of Madras became the seat of government.

On the 9th of December a French force of 1,700 men, almost entirely Europeans, of whom fifty were cavalry, two companies of Caffirs, six field-pieces, and six mortars, appeared before Fort St. David, and regularly invested it. The garrison, consisting of less than 200 men of the corps, assisted by some 2,000 badly armed and undisciplined natives, sallied out and drove the enemy back several miles, with a loss to the French of 150 men.

1747 Another unsuccessful attack was made by the French (who continued the investment) on the 19th of February 1747, when the garrison, having been reinforced by twenty recruits from England, marched out and gave them battle ; twelve English and twenty-two French were killed, and on the appearance of an English squadron in the offing the siege was raised. The squadron landed 100 European recruits, and shortly after 100 more men arrived from the Bombay Europeans (now our second battalion), a regiment raised by King Charles II in 1661, which landed in India in 1662, and was transferred to the East India Company in 1668.

Early in 1747 Mr., afterwards Lord Clive of Plassey, who also had escaped from Madras after its surrender, obtained a commission as ensign in the corps, which he at once joined, and assisted in the defence of Fort St. David.

1748 During this year the strength of the corps was 500 non-commissioned officers and men, and when the different companies were formed into a regular battalion a grenadier company was established. The men of the battalion, with the exception of the grenadiers, ceased to wear swords, and the officers carried, in addition to their swords, light fusils ; the serjeants, halberds.

CHAPTER II

MAJOR KNIPE, the commander of the garrison in Fort St. George, had died in May 1743, and after much delay the Court of Directors on the 17th of December 1746 selected Captain Stringer Lawrence, of the 14th Regiment of Foot, to succeed him, with a salary of £250 a year. Captain Lawrence was a distinguished officer who had seen much service in Spain and the Low Countries, and had been present during the rebellion of 1745 as adjutant to Lord Tyrawly. On the 18th February 1747, at the age of forty-nine years, he took the usual oath and sailed for India in the *Winchelsea*, with the rank of major.

1748 In January 1748 Major Lawrence, having with him 150 recruits, landed at Fort St. David, then momentarily expecting an attack from the French; he at once commenced to reorganise the seven independent companies of which the corps was then composed into an administrative regiment, to be known for the next hundred years as the ' Madras European Regiment,' and became its first colonel, retaining, however, the command and emoluments of one of the companies, viz. the grenadiers. In the following year (1749) the Bombay corps, now our second battalion, was also made a regular regiment.

In June, M. Dupleix, the French Governor-General, made another attempt against Cuddalore (a fortified town near Fort St. David), and on the 17th sent 800 French soldiers and 1,000 sepoys to attack it; but they were repulsed

MAJOR-GENERAL STRINGER LAWRENCE
The Regiment's first Colonel, 1748.

(From an Oil Painting by Sir J. Reynolds, in the possession of the Oriental Club, Hanover Square.)

with loss by the corps under Lawrence, the enemy never halting until within the boundary hedge of Trichinopoly.

On the 29th July Admiral Boscawen arrived with 1,200 infantry soldiers, volunteers from various regiments in England, and 200 Royal Artillerymen ; and on the 8th August the forces under Major Lawrence, consisting of 400 men of the Madras European Regiment, 70 artillerymen, 300 topasses (half-castes), 127 European volunteers, and 2,000 sepoys, joined those of the Admiral and marched to the siege of Pondicherry. With marines, sailors, and a Dutch contingent from Negapatam, the European rank and file amounted to 3,720 men. Lawrence's authority extended to the Company's troops alone, and they formed but a fifth of the whole force, not counting sepoys.

The whole of the operations by land and sea were in Boscawen's hands, and the subsequent miscarriage of affairs was ascribed to his ignorance of land warfare.

At the attack on the fort of Arriancopang, two miles from Pondicherry, the sailors were struck with panic at the sight of the enemy's cavalry and fled, and the panic com- municated itself to the rest of the troops. Lawrence, who commanded in the trenches, disdained to fly, was made a prisoner, and taken into Pondicherry. On the 30th August Boscawen broke ground before Pondicherry ; two sorties were made by the garrison, in repelling which the Madras European Regiment inflicted a severe loss on the enemy, and Ensign Clive particularly distinguished himself. On the 5th October Boscawen was compelled to raise the siege, having lost 1,000 of the Europeans of his force. The French lost 300 men only. In November news arrived of the cessation of arms in Europe, and Lawrence was released and permitted to return to Fort St. David on parole pending the treaty of Aix-la-Chapelle, which restored Madras to the English.

1749 Boscawen, burning to retrieve his disaster, determined to assist the Prince of Tanjore (who was under the East India Company's protection) against the French. He, consequently, at the end of March 1749 sent a force of 430 men of the Madras European Regiment, with 1,000 sepoys and a small siege train, under Captain Cope of the regiment, against Devi Cottah ; but after a series of blundering operations Cope was glad to make his way back to Fort St. David. A second expedition, however, was entrusted to Major Lawrence. This time success crowned our efforts, and it was on this occasion that Clive came prominently under Lawrence's notice. A breach had been made, and Clive volunteered to lead the storming party ; unfortunately, the sepoys of his detachment held back, which resulted in the little party of the corps with him being cut to pieces by the enemy's cavalry, Clive himself being the only one who escaped. Lawrence at once made a second assault at the head of the whole regiment, together with a detachment of the Bombay European Regiment, and 500 sepoys, and Devi Cottah fell with a loss of 300 to the enemy. Devi Cottah was then ceded to the English.

In August 1749 the English received back Madras from the French, but meanwhile, in the previous July the English decided to assist Mahomed Ali (known also as 'Wallajah '), the Nawab of the Carnatic, who was besieged at Trichinopoly by the French *protégé*, Chunda Sahib, and a strong French force. Accordingly, 120 men of the corps, with some officers, were sent to assist in the defence of that fortress.

In September 1749 many of the survivors of the force Boscawen had brought from England volunteered for the corps, as also eleven officers, amongst whom were John Dalton and James Kilpatrick, who subsequently greatly distinguished themselves in India.

1750 In February 1750 Lawrence marched to Pondicherry with 600 men of the corps to the assistance of the Soobah of the Deccan, who was opposed to the French and their nominee to the Soobahship, Moozuffer Jung (and also Chunda Sahib, their nominee to the Carnatic), and halted at Villanore, where he was declared generalissimo by the Soobah. The armies of the rival Soobahs, aided respectively by the French and English, came into action on the following day. Before a shot was fired on either side M. D'Auteuil, the French commander, sent a message to Lawrence acquainting him ' that although the two battalions (French and English) were engaged in different causes, yet it was not his design that any European blood should be spilt, but as he did not know the post of the British battalion, should any of his shot come that way he could not be blamed.' Lawrence replied ' that he had the honour of carrying the English colours on his flag gun, which, if he pleased to look out for, he might know from thence where the English were posted, but if any shots came that way, he might be assured he would return them.' Soon after, a shot was fired over the battalion, when three guns were instantly ordered to answer it, and Lawrence himself saw that they were well pointed. M. D'Auteuil seeing that Lawrence was not to be trifled with, and fearing the result of an action, retired during the night, and left eleven pieces of heavy artillery behind him. During this affair the corps was not engaged, but it heroically saved the abandoned French gunners from being cut to pieces by their enemies.

1751 In January 1751 Captain Cope was sent to Trichinopoly with 280 men of the corps and 300 sepoys. Madura was at that time in open revolt, and Captain Cope marched from Trichinopoly to reduce it, with 150 of the corps, one battering gun, three field-pieces, and two cohorns, accompanied by 600 of Mahomed Ali's cavalry.

An immediate attack on Madura was ordered ; the first wall was passed, and although the storming party had some difficulty in dispatching several of the enemy clothed in complete armour, yet the bayonet prevailed, the breach was mounted, and the parapet gained ; but owing to certain obstacles placed by the enemy in the ditch between the outer and inner walls through which they could thrust their long pikes, nearly every man who mounted was severely wounded ; and, in addition, the troops were exposed to the fire of some 4,000 matchlockmen.   Ninety of the corps being killed or wounded, and it being found impossible to advance further, the attack was relinquished, and Captain Cope, after destroying his battering gun, returned to Trichinopoly.

At this time intelligence was received that Chunda Sahib and the French were on their march from Arcot to besiege Trichinopoly, so that in April 1751, 450 of the corps (50 mounted as dragoons), 100 Caffirs, and 1,000 sepoys, with eight field-pieces, assembled at Fort St. David under Captain de Gingens, and in the following month being joined by Mahomed Ali's troops to the number of 600 horse and 1,000 peons, marched to Verdachellum, which surrendered.   Leaving there 30 of the corps and 50 sepoys as a garrison the force marched westwards, and being joined by an additional 100 men of the corps sent out by Captain Cope from Trichinopoly, together with 2,000 horse and 2,000 foot belonging to the Nawab Wallajah, arrived at Volcondah, which was assaulted and set fire to ; the British, however, owing to a strong reinforcement of Chunda Sahib's troops by the French, were eventually forced to retire, though with no loss.   Captains de Gingens, Dalton, Kilpatrick, and Lieutenant Clive of the corps were conspicuous for their good conduct and gallantry on the occasion.   The force then fell back towards Trichinopoly and took up a position at

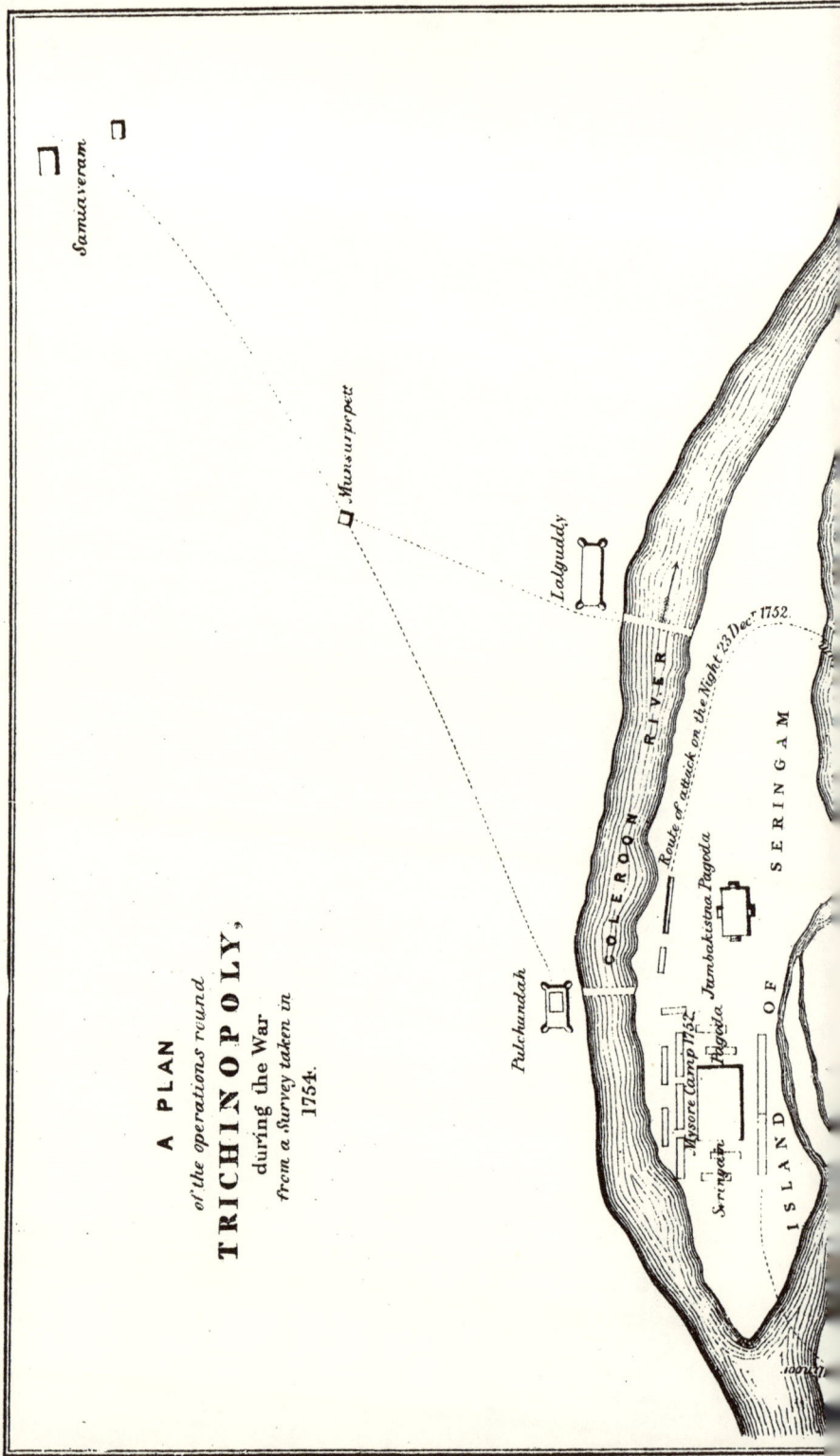

A PLAN

of the operations round

TRICHINOPOLY,

during the War

from a Survey taken in

1754.

Samiaveram.

Munsurpett

Lalguddy

Pulchundah

COLEROON RIVER

Route of attack on the Night 23 Dec 1752.

SERINGAM

Seringam

Pagoda

Jumbakistna Pagoda

Mysore Camp 1752

ISLAND OF

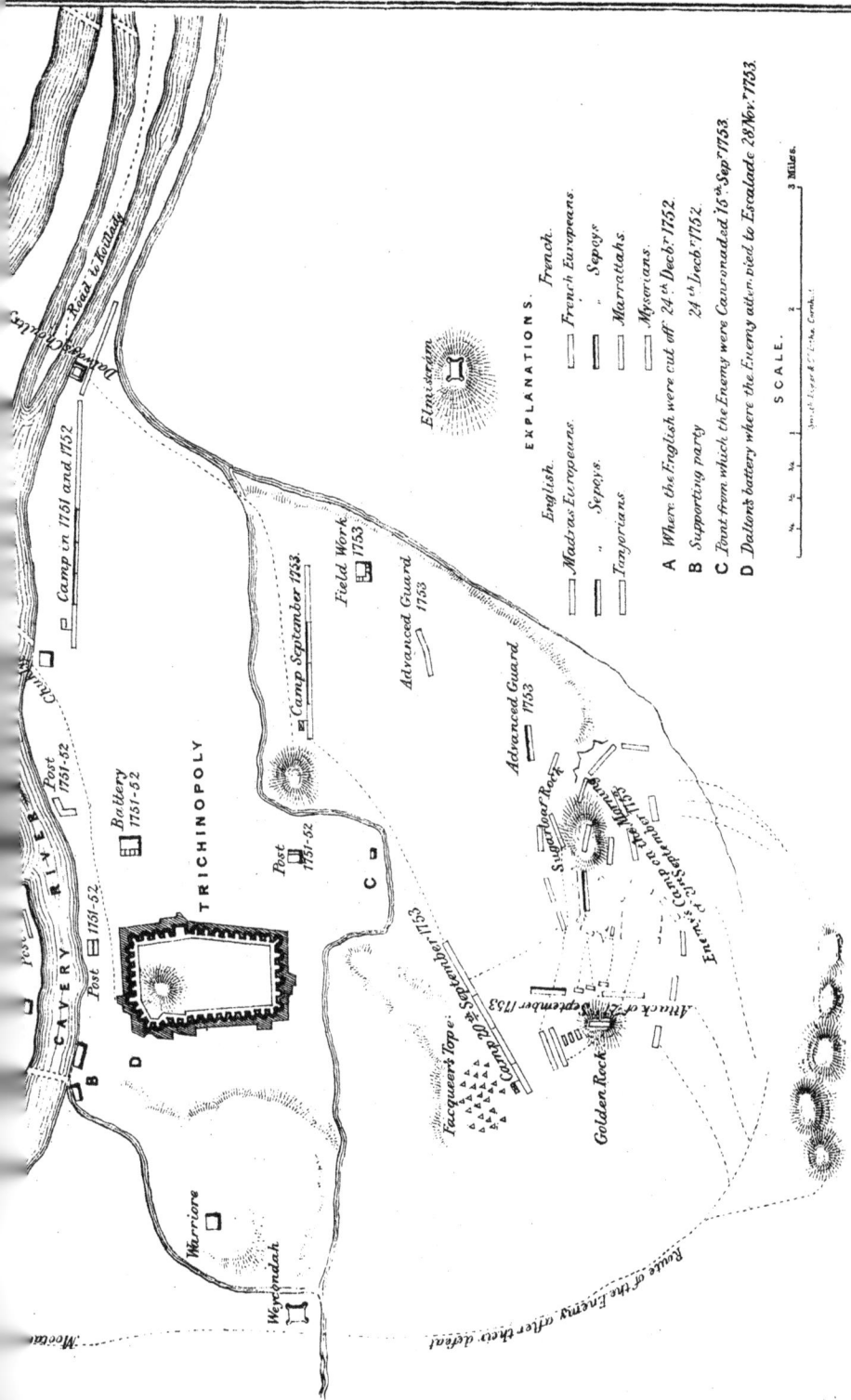

EXPLANATIONS.

English.   French.

Madras Europeans.   French Europeans.

Sepoys.   Sepoys.

Tanjorians.   Marrattahs.

                  Mysorians.

A   Where the English were cut off. 24ᵗʰ Decbʳ 1752.

B   Supporting party   24ᵗʰ Decbʳ 1752.

C   Point from which the Enemy were Cannonaded 15ᵗʰ Sepʳ 1753.

D   Dalton's battery where the Enemy adʳⁿ. vied to Escalade 28 Nov. 1753.

SCALE.

3 Miles.

Smith Royal & Cº Litho, Cornhill.

Elmiseram

Camp in 1751 and 1752

Road to Kistnah

Camp at Coilady

Post 1751-52

Battery 1751-52

Post 1751-52

TRICHINOPOLY

Post 1751-52

CAVERY RIVER

Camp Creek

Post

Camp September 1753

Field Work 1753

Advanced Guard 1753

Advanced Guard 1753

Advanced Guard 1753

Sugarloaf Rock

Enemy's Camp September 1753

Camp on 20ᵗʰ Sepr 1753

Facqueer's Tope

Camp 20ᵗʰ September 1753

C

D

B

Warriore

Weycondah

Meetoor

Golden Rock

Attack of 21ᵗʰ September 1753

Route of the Enemy after their defeat

Utatoor. Two days afterwards a body of 3,000 of the enemy's horse intercepted a small reconnoitring party headed by Captain de Gingens and seven of the officers of the corps. The party, consisting of twelve dragoons of the regiment and the above officers, charged through the horse sword in hand and all cut their way through except Lieutenant Maskelyne and three troopers, who were taken prisoners.

On the 15th July the grenadiers under Dalton greatly distinguished themselves, killing 300 of the enemy. On the 16th the force reached Trichinopoly, after which Lieutenant Clive was recalled to Fort St. David to conduct another reinforcement to Trichinopoly, and during the journey narrowly escaped capture. At Fort St. David he assumed charge of 100 men of the corps, 50 sepoys, and a small gun, and at the same time received his promotion to captain. On the march of the detachment to Trichinopoly, it was intercepted at Coiladdy by a force of 30 Frenchmen and 500 sepoys sent for that purpose; both parties suddenly met at the village of Gondore, a combat ensued in which all the French, including their commander and 100 of their sepoys, were destroyed, the rest dispersing and thus enabling Clive to reach Trichinopoly in safety.

Notwithstanding these augmentations the corps at Trichinopoly numbered only 600 men. The French could muster more than 900.

CHAPTER III

CAPTAIN CLIVE again returned to Madras from Trichinopoly, and on the suggestion of Major Stringer Lawrence, it was decided to attack Arcot and thereby create a diversion from beleaguered Trichinopoly. Clive **1751** was chosen for this duty, and on the 26th August, after 150 men of the corps had been left to garrison Forts St. George and St. David respectively, he marched towards Arcot with 200 of the corps and seven officers, one artillery subaltern, and 300 sepoys. This handful of men with three field-pieces arrived within ten miles of Arcot on the 31st, where the enemy's spies discovered them marching during a violent thunderstorm. This circumstance from the native opinion of omens discouraged the garrison of 1,100 men to such an extent that they instantly abandoned the fort, and Clive arriving shortly afterwards, marched through the city to the astonishment of about 100,000 inhabitants and took possession of it. Six hundred of the enemy's cavalry and 600 foot were, however, encamped at some distance from the fort. On both the 4th and 5th of September Clive attacked and defeated this body ; after which his men for ten days were busily engaged in repairing the defences and constructing necessary additions, during which they discovered large quantities of gunpowder and lead, eight guns from 4- to 8-pounders, and one large 72-pounder gun, said to have been sent by the Emperor Aurungzebe from Delhi, and represented as requiring 1,000 oxen to drag it. The

LORD CLIVE

Joined Regiment in 1747.

(From an oil painting by N. Dance, in the possession of the Oriental Club, Hanover Square.)

enemy, encouraged by the intermission of sallies and attributing the same to fear, became more confident and brought their camp three miles nearer to Arcot. Advantage was taken of their fancied security, and in an attack made on them on the night of the 14th September they were entirely routed and dispersed with much slaughter.

Meanwhile, Lawrence, having cause for dissatisfaction in regard to several matters connected with the adminis- tration of affairs by the Madras Council, resigned the Company's service on the 25th of September, and sailed for England a month later.

Two 18-pounders and military stores escorted by sepoys for the Arcot garrison being on the march, the enemy hoped to intercept them at Conjeveram, a celebrated Hindoo pagoda between Madras and Arcot; Clive sent thirty men of the corps and fifty sepoys to occupy the post, which, on their approach, was abandoned by the enemy. Much, however, depending on the safe arrival of the convoy, Clive, reserving thirty of the corps and fifty sepoys for the defence of Arcot, detached the rest of his force to bring it in. The enemy, thinking to gain possession of Arcot during the absence of the greater part of the garrison, suddenly attacked it in the evening, kept up a brisk fire and twice attempted to force the gates, but they were invariably repulsed with severe loss, and on the approach of the convoy on the following morning they retreated with precipitation.

The taking of Arcot had the desired effect. Chunda Sahib immediately dispatched from Trichinopoly 4,000 troops under his son Rajah Sahib, which were joined by 150 French soldiers from Pondicherry; these arriving on the 23rd September occupied the town and regularly invested the fort. On the 24th September Clive, at the head of his garrison, made a sortie towards the Nawab's palace, which was situated close to the walls of the fort, in front of which,

with four guns, the French troops were drawn up ; these
being driven from their guns at the point of the bayonet
ran into the palace, where they kept up so severe a fire of
musketry that fourteen men of the corps, who tried to bring
away the captured guns, were killed or wounded. The
British after cannonading the palace retired with their guns
to the fort. A party under Lieutenant Glass of the corps
had dispersed a large body of sepoys at the same time in
another direction. The loss during these operations was
fifteen men of the corps, who were either killed or died
shortly after of their wounds, and Lieutenant Trenwith, who
was shot through the body. Lieutenant Revel, the artillery
officer, and sixteen other men were disabled.

The following day 2,000 men from Vellore joined the
enemy and took possession of all the streets and avenues
leading to the fort.

The fort of Arcot was about a mile in circumference, the
walls in many places ruinous, the ramparts too weak and
narrow to permit the firing of artillery, the parapet low
and slightly built, the towers mostly decayed and none
capable of receiving more than one piece of ordnance, the
ditch was in most places fordable, in many dry and choked
up, the gateways were solid projections of masonry, and
instead of a drawbridge, the ditch had a large causeway
built across it.

At the end of September, quite early in the siege, the
services of four out of the eight officers were lost : one being
killed, two wounded, and one dispatched to Madras. The
troops fit for duty were diminished to 120 men of the corps
and 200 sepoys, these being opposed to 150 Frenchmen,
2,000 sepoys, 5,000 peons, and 3,000 cavalry.

There being in the fort provisions for sixty days only, all
the native inhabitants were turned out until the 24th October.
The fort was bombarded by four mortars, two 18-pounders,

and seven smaller guns, and in six days a practicable breach fifty feet wide was made in the curtain of the north-west wall. The garrison constructed entrenchments behind it, and planted artillery for its defence, at the same time mounting the 72-pounder gun on one of the towers ; this was daily fired with a charge of thirty-two pounds of powder at the Nawab's palace, which created some alarm in the town, but on the fourth day the gun burst. The enemy also mounted a gun on the roof of a house, but a few rounds from an 18-pounder knocked the house down, and under its ruins some fifty of the enemy were killed or injured.

Government being anxious to relieve Arcot, a reinforce-ment of 100 of the corps and 200 sepoys, under Lieutenant Innes, was dispatched from Madras and proceeded as far as Trivatore, when they were surrounded by 2,000 natives, 20 French soldiers, and two guns, sent from Arcot to inter-cept them. Lieutenant Innes charged and took the enemy's guns with a loss of twenty men and two officers of the corps killed, and a great many wounded. The enemy were repulsed and suffered heavily, but the detachment had to return to Poonamallee, at that time a frontier fort of the Company.

On the south-west side Arcot had also been breached, and Lieutenant Innes's retreat left the garrison little hope of succour from Madras. Captain Clive having strengthened this breach as he had done the other, returned an answer of defiance to an offer of terms made by Rajah Sahib. The enemy, therefore, determined upon an immediate storm, which, on the morning of the 14th November, took place. Two divisions advanced to the gates and two to the breaches, with a multitude besides, who attempted to escalade the numerous parts of the wall which were accessible. The columns which attacked the gates drove in front of them several elephants protected with armour on their heads for the purpose of pushing them open. These elephants being wounded by musketry and hand grenades became unmanageable, and trampled down the storming party in their rear, who dispersed and sought safety in flight. The division attacking the north-west breach crossed the ditch, which was fordable, and in a few moments the *fausse braye* was crowded with the enemy, who mounted the breach with the greatest intrepidity, which they were suffered to approach and crowd with impunity before the defenders opened fire, when it fell with fearful execution, every shot telling ; the field-pieces, also, kept up continued discharges, but as soon as one body of the enemy was driven back and destroyed another immediately crowded to the assault, until some bombs, thrown into the *fausse braye*, bursting, destroyed many, and drove the rest away from the breach and over the ditch. At the breach to the south-west the enemy brought a raft, on which nearly 100 embarked, but after a few rounds of grape it was capsized ; several of the men were drowned or killed, and the rest were driven to the other side. The attack continued for upwards of an hour, after which the enemy suddenly desisted and employed themselves in carrying off their dead ; amongst these was the sepoy commander, who had distinguished himself with great bravery during the storm. Two hours later the enemy again opened a heavy fire of musketry and cannon. At 2 P.M. they requested leave to bury their dead, which was allowed, and a truce granted until 4 P.M., when they again recommenced their fire and continued it until 2 A.M. the following morning, after which it ceased entirely. At daybreak it was discovered they had abandoned the town. The garrison then immediately marched out and took four pieces of artillery, four mortars, and a large quantity of ammunition abandoned by the enemy.

Thus, after fifty days, ended the siege of Arcot, during which 45 men of the corps and 30 sepoys were killed, and a greater number of both wounded. On the day of the assault there were but 80 men of the corps, including officers, and 120 sepoys, to repel it, in doing which their loss was only four of the corps killed and two sepoys wounded. The loss of the enemy was upwards of 400 killed.

Among the numerous gallant and desperate services any part of the corps has ever, at any period of its existence, been engaged in, the defence of Arcot must always rank as one reflecting the most honour upon it. The sepoys, too, rivalled their European comrades in feats of daring, and when provisions became so scarce that it was feared famine might compel a surrender, they came forward and offered Clive to take, as their share of food, the water in which the rice was boiled, saying it was sufficient for their support, but that Europeans required the grain, which was more nourishing.

CHAPTER IV

ON the evening of the day on which the siege of Arcot was raised a party of 250 men, and four guns, arrived under the command of Captain Kilpatrick of the corps. On the 19th November, Clive, leaving **1751** Kilpatrick with a garrison in the fort, took the field with 200 of the corps, 700 sepoys, and three guns, and marched to Timery, which surrendered. The Mahrattas having joined Clive with 600 horse, he made a forced march of twenty miles and encountered the enemy as they were preparing to cross the river north of Arnee. The enemy, numbering 300 French soldiers, 2,500 sepoys, 2,000 horse, and four guns, immediately they perceived the English, advanced to the attack. Clive drew up in position, the sepoys on the right, the Mahratta cavalry on the left, and the men of the corps, with the guns, in the centre. An engagement ensued ; the enemy retired in confusion, and being followed up took shelter within and under the walls of Arnee. Fifty Frenchmen and 150 of their sepoys were killed ; the English lost no Europeans and only eight sepoys; the Mahrattas suffered a loss of 50 men.

The next day the enemy retreated to Gingee.

On entering the town of Arnee the corps captured many tents, a large quantity of baggage, an elephant, and several horses. The Mahratta cavalry continued the pursuit, and returned before night with 400 horses, quantities of plunder, and the enemy's cash chest, containing 100,000 rupees. Many of the enemy's sepoys then came in and offered their services ; Clive enlisted 600 of them.

During the siege, the French had occupied Conjeveram with 300 Frenchmen and 300 sepoys, thus interrupting communication with Madras, and surprising a number of disabled men returning from Arcot, amongst others, Lieutenants Glass and Revel, and six men of the corps ; the officers were spared, but the six soldiers were barbarously murdered in their litters. Captain Clive three days after his victory marched thither and summoned the French officer, but he, not understanding English, desired his prisoners to write that ' if his post was attacked he would expose them on the works.' This the officers wrote, but pressed Clive to attack instantly. On the arrival of two battering guns from Madras Clive began to batter the walls; the garrison returned a hot fire which killed Lieutenant Bulkley and several men of the corps, but fearing the resentment of the English the enemy abandoned their post during the night and escaped. After destroying the defences of Conjeveram, Clive sent 200 men of the corps and 500 sepoys back to Arcot, and in the middle of December returned with the rest to Madras.

While one part of the corps was carrying on war in the Arcot provinces, another part was upholding the honour and credit of the service in a number of gallant combats near Trichinopoly, which the French and Chunda Sahib continued to invest.

The city of Trichinopoly is situated on a plain, its walls are nearly four miles in circumference, and a rock 300 feet high stands in the middle, which was of the utmost use to the British during the war. It is bounded on the east by the Tanjore country, on the south by that of the Tondiman, or chief of the Poligars, and to the north by the Coleroon river. The different rocks on the plain a few miles south of the fort were repeatedly the scenes of hard-fought battles, especially the Golden and Sugar Loaf Rocks to the south, and the French Rock to the west of the city walls. Captain de Gingens, who was in command, was an officer of proved courage who had seen much service in Europe before he entered the corps, but he prudently preserved the few men under him, allowing the enemy to exhaust their means and resources while saving his own, and awaited reinforcements from Arcot. Several gallant actions were, however, fought in the neighbourhood, in which the grenadiers of the corps, under Dalton, greatly distinguished themselves.

After the reduction of Conjeveram, the enemy still continuing their depredations, and even plundering the country up to St. Thomas's Mount, near Madras, and the gates of Poonamallee, it was determined to reduce and disperse them before advancing to Trichinopoly, and Clive was put in command of 380 of the corps, 1,300 sepoys, with six field-guns, for this purpose.

1752   Clive left Fort St. George on the 22nd February 1752, and found the enemy entrenched at Vendalore, twenty-five miles from Madras. On the approach of the English they fled, and marched in haste to Arcot, hoping that the English sepoys in garrison there would betray their trust; but in this they were disappointed, and an attack they made on the gateways was repulsed. Clive rapidly followed, on the way took Conjeveram, and arrived at sunset at Cauveripauk, where he suddenly found himself ambuscaded by the enemy, and his van fired on at 200 yards' distance by nine pieces of artillery. The British sustained some loss; the baggage was sent to the rear, and the infantry took up a position in a watercourse. A bright moon was shining while a heavy fire was kept up by the enemy for two hours, but as it could only be answered by three British guns it did great execution, and either killed or disabled so many of the artillerymen that it became imperative either to take the enemy's guns or to retreat. A serjeant of the corps named Shawlum was sent with two sepoys to reconnoitre; he reported that no troops were posted in rear of the enemy's guns, on which 200 men of the corps and 400 sepoys were at once detached under Lieutenant Keene of the corps, with the serjeant as their guide, to take the guns in reverse.

Keene's party got unperceived to within 300 yards of the enemy's artillery when Ensign Simmons, who was sent forward to reconnoitre, suddenly came across a watercourse full of sepoys, but as he replied to them in French he was permitted to pass, when, having seen that the guns were protected by 100 French soldiers who were looking out towards their front, he returned, and having conducted the party to within thirty yards of the artillery, a well-directed volley, followed up by a charge, swept the French from their guns and entirely routed them; a few, however, surrendered.

The enemy in front no sooner saw their artillery silenced than they dispersed, the English remaining under arms until daylight, when they found 60 Frenchmen, prisoners, and 50 dead on the field, besides 300 sepoys. The guns captured were nine field-pieces and three mortars. Of the corps 40 were killed and upwards of 60 wounded. This victory destroyed the French force in that quarter and established the reputation of British arms in India, besides convincing the natives that the British, as soldiers, were superior to the French.

On the return of the detachment to Fort St. David it passed through the spot where Nazir Jung had been assassinated, and where a town had been built by the French, to which the name ' Dupleix Tatha Bad ' (Dupleix's Town of Victory) had been given; a pillar had also been erected commemorating in every language events deemed by them as victories. Clive and his troops razed this to the ground, and afterwards marched to the Presidency.

Three days after their arrival at Fort St. David part of the corps was ready to take the field under Clive for the relief of Trichinopoly, which had been beleaguered for seven months by Chunda Sahib and a French army under M. Law, when, on the 15th March, Major Lawrence arrived from England, and two days afterwards placed himself at its head.

Lawrence's resignation had not been accepted, and before he had been two months in England the directors sent him back with the appointment of Commander-in-Chief of all the Company's military forces in the East Indies, on a salary of £750 per annum ; he was also commissioned to consider the proper establishment for forming a company of artillery at Fort St. George.

Major Lawrence thus became the first Commander-in-Chief of the Indian Army.

On the 17th March Lawrence, with 400 of the corps, 1,100 sepoys, eight field-pieces, and a large quantity of stores, marched for Trichinopoly. On the 27th he passed under the guns of the fort of Coiladdy, on the Coleroon river east of Trichinopoly, which was held by the enemy, but owing to ignorance or treachery on the part of his guides and before he could withdraw, he suffered a loss of twenty men of the corps killed and wounded ; the march, however, was continued to within ten miles of Trichinopoly without further opposition, when a halt was called for the night.

To this spot Captain de Gingens had sent the same night a reinforcement of 100 men and 50 dragoons, all of the corps, and early next morning, the 28th March, Dalton with his grenadiers, and a battalion company under Captain Clarke, in all 200 of the corps, 400 sepoys, and four guns, were ordered to the Sugar Loaf Rock and to remain there until the convoy came in sight, when they were to join it. Lawrence then advanced, and found the enemy drawn up, their right resting on the village of Chuckle-polliam near the Cauvery, and their left on the inaccessible and fortified rock of Elmiseram, round which he moved, covering his baggage which was on his left flank.

Near the Sugar Loaf Rock he was met by Dalton, accompanied by the Nawab's army and the Mahrattas, whose cavalry pretended to skirmish in the plain. It being then noon and the sun very hot, the troops were halted for refreshment, but in an hour's time the enemy advanced to the attack. The grenadiers instantly occupied a small choultry, as did also the first division of artillery. The French battalion advancing to dislodge them were severely handled and kept in check until the rest of the force came up, followed by the Mysore and Mahratta allies at a distance, they being afraid to expose their horses.

A cannonade began from twenty-two French guns against nine of the English; but the fire of the latter did the most execution, as they were sheltered by the choultry, whereas the enemy's guns were exposed on the open plain.

After a time the French battalion began to waver and ultimately retired, followed by their allies.

Captains Clive and Dalton continued the pursuit until the French were thrown into confusion and dispersed, when Lawrence recalled them, unwilling longer to expose his men to the excessive heat. Twenty-three men of the corps were killed, seven of these from sunstroke, and 30 were wounded.

The enemy left 40 Europeans, 300 of Chunda Sahib's troops, including their commander, 280 horses, and one elephant, dead on the plain.

Lawrence the same night proceeded with his convoy and deposited it in the fortress of Trichinopoly.

c 2

CHAPTER V

L AWRENCE lost no time in again harassing the enemy, and on the night of the 29th March he sent Dalton with 400 of the corps to beat up the French camp and set it on fire. Dalton lost his way, but **1752** managed to regain Trichinopoly without loss, though morning had surprised him in the midst of the French posts.

The mere attempt, however, alarmed Law to such an extent that he at once withdrew across the south bank of the Cauvery to the island of Seringham.

On the 30th, Dalton, with 100 grenadiers and some sepoys, attacked Elmiseram, an isolated rock with a fortified temple on its summit, which he took with a loss of only five men of the corps. The garrison of fifteen French and thirty sepoys were taken prisoners, and some guns and a fine 18-pounder were captured, the latter being presented to the Nawab Wallajah as the first piece of ordnance captured during the campaign.

On the 2nd April the grenadiers, always remarkable for great spirit and gallantry, attacked at noon a battery in the enemy's camp in Seringham, took a large gun and brought it across the river and into Trichinopoly, in the face of their entire army.

Lawrence now decided to divide his forces, with the object of compelling the enemy to quit their ground.

On the 6th April he sent Clive with 400 of the corps,

700 sepoys, 3,000 Mahrattas, 1,000 Tanjore horse, and six field-pieces, with two battering guns, north of the Coleroon to intercept the enemy's communications with Pondicherry. The position chosen was Samiaveram, seven miles north of the river, where two pagodas were occupied and strongly entrenched. On the 7th April Munserpett was attacked and captured with a loss of one officer and three men of the corps killed. On the 8th the fort of Lalguddi was taken and the magazine of provisions it contained destroyed or carried off.

On the 14th April Clive marched on Utatoor to intercept a French convoy from Pondicherry, but the enemy retreated and Clive returned to Samiaveram. On the afternoon of the 15th April the French heard of his departure from Samiaveram and thought to surprise the post during his absence; they therefore sent 80 Frenchmen and 700 sepoys to attack it, who arrived at midnight, and having answered the challenge in English, were allowed by our sepoys to advance to the smaller pagoda, where, being again challenged, they fired a volley into the guard-rooms and choultry, in the latter of which Clive was sleeping. They then rushed into the pagoda and bayonetted all they met. Clive, starting from his sleep, hurried to the larger pagoda, where the men of the corps there quartered had taken the alarm, and were under arms.

Seeing a large body of sepoys drawn up and firing at random, their confusion confirmed his belief that they were his own men. The men of the corps were therefore placed twenty paces in their rear, and Clive went forward to order them to cease their fire. A French sepoy, perceiving that he was an English officer, attacked and wounded him in two places. Following the sepoy to the gate he was accosted by a French officer and six men, when, retaining his self-possession, he informed the Frenchman that his

detachment was surrounded and that no quarter would
be given unless he instantly surrendered, on which the
party laid down their arms and followed him to the large
pagoda, to which he hastened, to order the corps to attack
the sepoys, but on arrival found that they (the sepoys)
had marched off unmolested, the soldiers of the corps
thinking them to be English sepoys.

Whilst Clive was giving directions to his men a party
of eight Frenchmen came up and were instantly seized,
and with those already taken were marched off to the
small pagoda under escort.   On arriving there, however,
it was found to be in possession of the enemy ; the escort,
therefore, were at once made prisoners, and the French
released.

Clive being informed of this determined to attack
the small pagoda, and a party moved off at once to the
assault, which, however, was beaten back with the loss of
an officer and fifteen men of the corps ; but the enemy
making a sally immediately after were received so warmly
that their officer and twenty men were struck down, and
the rest retired into the pagoda.   Clive then going forward
to parley was fired at, and two serjeants on whom he
was leaning were shot dead ; the enemy then surrendered.

The Mahratta cavalry pursued the retiring enemy,
and not one of the 700 sepoys escaped—they were all killed
to a man.

Of the entire French detachment which entered Samiaveram not a man returned ; and although the affair of the
15th April was one of the most extraordinary, and from
first to last a series of blunders and mistakes, costing the
English in repelling it many valuable lives, yet the serious
loss to the enemy of fully 800 good troops was as severe a
blow as had been inflicted during the war.

The French post at Utatoor, where the convoy remained

awaiting an opportunity to enter Seringham, was, to them, a most important one; consequently, on the 9th May, Dalton with the grenadiers and a battalion company of the corps, in all 150 men, 400 sepoys, and 500 Mahratta cavalry, with four guns, marched to attack it.

On Dalton's advance, after some outpost fighting and the loss of an officer of the corps mortally wounded, the enemy were driven into the fort, which, however, the French under M. D'Auteuil evacuated during the night, making a rapid retreat to Volcondah.

The French at Seringham under M. Law, supposing that Dalton's detachment was part of Clive's force at Samiaveram, crossed over to attack it on the 11th May, but Clive advancing to meet them, they at once retired.

Dalton remained two days at Utatoor and then joined Clive, who determined to attack Pitchanda, which kept up the enemy's communications with the country north of the Coleroon river; six guns were also placed for the cannonading of Seringham on the island.

Pitchanda surrendered after losing several men killed, also fifteen Frenchmen, who jumped into the river and were drowned.

Most of Chunda Sahib's officers and men then in Seringham now deserted him; 2,000 of his best horse and 1,500 foot joined Clive, and the rest returned to their homes. Chunda Sahib withdrew within the pagoda with no more than 2,000 horse, 3,000 foot, and 1,000 Rajpoots. The French at this time occupied the Jumba Kistna Pagoda.

On the 18th May the French withdrew inside the pagoda, and Lawrence commenced his investment.

Meanwhile, it was important that the French convoy should be destroyed; it had taken shelter at Volcondah, and was again advancing.

For this purpose Clive marched on the evening of the 27th May with 100 of the corps, 1,000 sepoys, 1,000 Mahratta horse, and six guns, and next morning came up with the enemy at Volcondah. Clive then advanced and prepared to batter in the gate, when M. D'Auteuil hung out the white flag, and terms were soon settled; 100 Frenchmen, 400 sepoys, and 340 horse surrendered. Three guns, three large magazines containing military stores, 800 barrels of powder, and 3,000 muskets were found in the pettah, as also a sum of 50,000 rupees. The booty secured was valued at £10,000. The native prisoners were discovered and set at liberty, but Clive returned to his camp with the French soldiers and booty on the 30th May.

On the following day Chunda Sahib surrendered to our ally Manockjee, the Tanjore general, who at once had him stabbed to the heart, and his head being severed was sent to Mahomed Ali, who then for the first time saw the face of his enemy.

On the 3rd June the French forces under M. Law surrendered themselves as prisoners of war to Major Stringer Lawrence; they numbered 800 French soldiers, 35 officers, and 2,000 sepoys. Four mortars, eight cohorns, and 31 guns, besides large quantities of stores fell into the hands of the British at the same time.

Four hundred of the French prisoners were escorted into Fort St. David by Captain Campbell of the corps; the rest, with the artillery and stores, were taken into Trichinopoly. A portion of the corps then marched to Trivadi under Lawrence, who shortly afterwards went to Fort St. David for his health, leaving the command to Captain de Gingens.

In the latter end of July the French, having received large reinforcements from Europe, prepared to take the field.

A force consisting of 500 Frenchmen, 1,500 sepoys, and 500 horse, under M. de Kerjean, marched from Pondicherry and encamped within a short distance to the north of Fort St. David, on which, the portion of the corps at Trivadi marched out and encamped not far from that fort.

On the 16th August Lawrence arrived with a reinforcement and joined the force, which then amounted to 400 of the corps, 1,700 sepoys, eight guns, and 4,000 of the Nawab's troops, horse and foot.

The French retreated, but after some manœuvring the rival armies met at Bahoor. The sepoys on the British side formed the first line, the corps the second, with the artillery on its flanks, the Nawab's troops on the flanks of both lines.

The English advanced to the attack before daylight on the 26th August, and their sepoys coming into contact with those of the French, a heavy fire was kept up till day began to dawn, when the French battalion was discovered drawn up fronting that of the corps. After exchanging a hot fire, the grenadiers of the corps and two platoon companies forced their way through the French line, which had stood the shock for a time, both lines crossing bayonets without flinching—a circumstance almost unprecedented in war. The enemy then dispersed in all directions, throwing away their arms in their flight.

Upwards of 100 of the French fell by the bayonet alone, besides many others who were killed or wounded by the fire. M. de Kerjean, the commander-in-chief, thirteen officers, and upwards of 100 men were taken prisoners, and had the Nawab's cavalry done their duty not one of the enemy could have escaped. All the French guns (fourteen field-pieces), ammunition, and baggage were taken.

The battle of Bahoor was one of the very few actions on record in modern warfare where two corps of about the same strength, after a hot fire, both simultaneously advanced to the charge and actually met and crossed bayonets, and it was not until after some minutes' hard fighting, when the English corps broke through the centre of the French line, that it gave way. From the loss sustained by the corps, viz. one officer killed, four wounded, and seventy-eight men killed and wounded, mostly by bayonet thrusts, the resistance made by the enemy was evidently of a most determined and gallant character.

CHAPTER VI

AFTER the victory of Bahoor Lawrence recommended the reduction of Chingleyput and Covelong, and a force of 200 recruits of the corps lately landed, and 500 undisciplined sepoys, was sent from Madras for that purpose, under Clive, who volunteered to command it.

1752

On the 10th September the party marched against Covelong with four 24-pounders. Before, however, the guns had been placed in battery the fort surrendered; but next morning the detachment marched out to meet a party of the enemy advancing to the relief of the place, and suddenly falling upon them delivered their fire with such execution that upwards of 100 men were knocked over by the first volley, and in a charge that instantly followed the French commander, 25 French soldiers, and 250 sepoys were taken prisoners, and two guns were captured; the rest of the enemy flung away their arms and fled to Chingleyput, whither Clive immediately followed them. On arrival the guns were opened and a breach made in the outer wall, when, on the 31st October, the fort surrendered. Chingleyput was then garrisoned by the English.

Clive's health at this time broke down and he embarked for England in November, not returning to India until October 1755.

After Dalton was left by Lawrence in command at Trichinopoly in June, he had a considerable amount

of trouble with his so-called Mysorean allies : on one
occasion losing twenty men of the corps killed and wounded
owing to their treachery, and on the 25th December he
was exposed to the sudden attack of 4,000 horse, who
sabred 70 men of the corps and 300 of the best sepoys,
but a disaster was averted by the rest of the force steadily
covering the retreat into Trichinopoly.

On the 30th December a small party of the corps
attacked and carried a strongly fortified post called Ullore,
putting the garrison to the sword. The following day
Dalton resolved to confine his exertions to the defence
of Trichinopoly alone.

1753   From this time until the end of March Trichinopoly was closely invested ; provisions were
running short, and Dalton had been forced to send an
express to Lawrence asking for assistance. The intelligence of Trichinopoly's straitened circumstances reached
Lawrence at Trivadi at ten o'clock at night on the 20th
April.

Leaving 650 men at Trivadi, 150 of whom belonged
to the corps, he, without orders from Government, marched
at six hours' notice to Fort St. David to collect supplies ;
marching again next day he entered Trichinopoly on the
6th May—the seventeenth day from the receipt of Dalton's
message. His whole force, including the original garrison,
consisted only of 500 of the corps, 2,000 sepoys, and 3,000 of
the Nawab's horse. His artillery comprised ten field-pieces
and two 18-pounders.

Directly Lawrence withdrew from Trivadi, M. Dupleix
dispatched M. Astruc with 200 French soldiers, 500 sepoys,
and four guns to Trichinopoly.

Astruc joined the Mysoreans at Seringham the day
after Lawrence arrived, and assumed command of the
whole force on the island.

Lawrence was badly off for supplies and at a great disadvantage through want of cavalry; he therefore abandoned the idea of dislodging the enemy from Seringham, and devoted himself to procuring provisions. For this purpose he encamped at the Fakeers Tope, two and a half miles from the city, so as to prevent a complete investment, and sent out foraging parties. In this position he remained five weeks without being able to bring the French to action, and with very scanty supplies.

Meanwhile, affairs were going very badly for the English in other parts of the Carnatic. Trivadi with the force left in it was captured by the French; a similar mishap occurred at Arcot; every petty chieftain or soldier of fortune ravaged the territories which gave allegiance to Mahomed Ali, the Nawab Wallajah.

Dupleix, whose sole views were centred on Trichinopoly and the capture of Mahomed Ali, discouraged the Mahrattas from partaking in the general plunder and prevailed on them to join M. Astruc, to whom he sent 300 additional French soldiers and 1,000 sepoys.

On receipt of these reinforcements M. Astruc crossed the Cauvery and encamped near Weycondah west of the city. His force consisted of 450 French soldiers, 1,500 well-trained sepoys, 11,500 Mysore and Mahratta horse, under Hyder Ali and Morari Row respectively, two companies of topasses (half-caste Portuguese), and 1,200 Mysore sepoys, as also a nondescript rabble of 15,000 footmen variously armed.

Lawrence had at his disposal 500 men of the corps, 2,000 sepoys, of whom 700 were absent obtaining supplies, and 100 of the Nawab's horse.

Two miles south-west of the Fakeers Tope were some rocky hills known as the Five Rocks, where Lawrence maintained a sepoy guard, which, through the disobedience of the commander during Lawrence's temporary absence in the city, had been withdrawn.

Astruc occupying this post during the night advanced his guns and bombarded the English camp. Lawrence maintained his position during the day, and at night withdrew his camp behind a slight eminence nearer the city. Astruc then brought his whole force to the Five Rocks, cutting off Lawrence from his source of supplies, and from his absent 700 sepoys who were collecting rice in the Tondiman's country.

Lawrence's position was full of peril. Half a mile from his camp and nearly a mile from Astruc's was the Golden Rock, where Lawrence had posted a guard of 200 sepoys.

At daybreak on the 26th June Astruc attacked it with a mixed force of Europeans and sepoys, and in spite of a gallant resistance overwhelmed the defenders, killing or taking prisoners the whole of them.

The French battalion was then brought up behind the Rock and the French guns were posted at the base and opened fire ; the whole Mysore army was drawn up about a cannon shot in rear, while the Mahratta cavalry threatened the flanks and rear of the small English force.

Lawrence's position was truly desperate : 700 of his sepoys were absent, 200 more had just been destroyed, and after providing for the safety of his camp he could only muster 300 men of the corps, 80 artillerymen, and 500 sepoys.

With this force he had advanced to within a short distance of the Golden Rock before the outpost was overwhelmed. To retreat in face of the numerous horsemen and pressed by Astruc's Frenchmen meant probable destruction, yet to attack a strong position held by such an overwhelming force seemed nothing but sheer madness.

Lawrence chose the heroic part; his officers agreed in the wisdom of attacking, while the men expressed their delight in having ' a knock at the Frenchmen ' who had kept so long out of reach.

Ordering the grenadier company to assault the Rock, Lawrence moved with the rest of his little force round the base of it to attack the French battalion.

Seldom in war has such a sight been seen as this little band of British soldiers moving to the attack surrounded by many thousands of enemies. Scrambling up the Rock with fixed bayonets and without pulling a trigger, cheering as they moved, the unexpected onset of the grenadiers, led by Captains Kirk and Kilpatrick, struck the French defenders with panic, and not daring to stand the shock they fled headlong down the reverse side.

Meanwhile Astruc, behind the Rock not seeing what had happened, wheeled up his battalion to meet Lawrence, thus exposing his right flank to the fire of the grenadiers from the Rock. At this moment Lawrence drew up his men directly opposite the French front at twenty yards' distance.

In spite of M. Astruc's efforts, his men were struck with consternation at seeing themselves attacked by the foe that a few moments before had seemed in their power; smitten by musketry in front and flank they fell into disorder, which a bayonet charge preceded by a volley converted into a panic, and they fled from the field, leaving three guns in Lawrence's hands.

In vain the Mahrattas strove to retrieve the fortunes of the day (some of the corps fell under their sabres while in disorder taking possession of the guns), but they were soon forced to withdraw with the loss of many men.

The French then rallied on the Mysore army and contented themselves with keeping up an ineffectual cannonade. For three hours Lawrence remained at the foot of the

Rock in the expectation that they would renew the combat, and then finding that the French would not advance, he formed his little army into a hollow square, with the captured guns and about seventy prisoners in the centre, and deliberately marched back towards his camp.

Hardly had he got clear of the Rock when the whole of the enemy's cavalry, upwards of 10,000 in number, charged furiously down. The square was halted and the guns run out at the angles and rapidly served, the men also pouring volleys into the dense masses whenever they approached, as they frequently did, close to the points of the bayonets, till, after losing some 600 of their number, the enemy broke up and forsook the field, leaving the little band of heroes to march unmolested back to camp, bearing with them their trophies of victory. No finer feat of arms was ever performed. The first result of this victory was to produce dissension between the French and their allies; M. Astruc, also, made over command to M. Brenier, and repaired to Pondicherry.

Lawrence, having secured fifty days' provisions and leaving Dalton with a small garrison in Trichinopoly, marched on the 2nd July towards Tanjore, his objects being to induce the Tanjore chief to furnish him with cavalry, and to meet a reinforcement on its way from the coast.

M. Brenier closely invested the city, but could not summon sufficient resolution to assault it, Dalton's vigilance, together with occasional sorties, preventing any such attempt.

It was about this time that the corps obtained the soubriquet of ' The Lambs.'

CHAPTER VII

MEANWHILE Lawrence had gained over the Tanjore chief, who furnished him with 3,000 horse and 2,000 matchlockmen ; he also received a reinforcement of **1753** 170 men of the corps and 300 sepoys from Fort St. David. With his force thus increased Lawrence arrived within ten miles of Trichinopoly.

Brenier determined to intercept him, and occupied the strong positions south of the city from Weycondah to Elmiseram : the centre of the whole being the Golden and Sugar Loaf Rocks, about half a mile apart, which were held in force by the French infantry and artillery.

On the 9th August Lawrence resumed his advance, but encumbered with thousands of bullocks it appeared impossible to force a passage ; he had, however, the advantage of an exact knowledge of Brenier's forces communicated to him by Dalton.

The key of the French position was the Golden Rock. Lawrence formed up his men as if he intended to attack the Sugar Loaf Rock ; Brenier fell into the trap and denuded the Golden Rock to strengthen the point threatened. Lawrence thereupon detached his grenadier company with 800 sepoys to seize the Golden Rock—a movement not perceived by the French till too late to prevent it.

Brenier then sent 300 Frenchmen to strengthen the small party left at the Golden Rock, and 100 cavalry to hamper the English infantry on their way. But the

D

grenadiers were not to be delayed; without halting they kept up a rolling fire on the cavalry, who refrained from closing, till reaching the Golden Rock they drove the enemy down and planted their colours on the summit before the French infantry could reach the spot.

This party of the enemy then took post on some high ground between the two rocks and opened a galling fire from four guns on the Golden Rock.

Brenier instead of advancing remained halted near the Sugar Loaf Rock, while Lawrence moved his whole force, convoy and all, to the Golden Rock. An artillery duel ensued in which the English regiment suffered some loss; but at this juncture Dalton issued from the city with two field-pieces and his detachment, in rear of the enemy's cavalry, who at once galloped off.

Lawrence then sent the grenadiers and 200 more of the corps, with 300 sepoys, against the French detachment, who received them with a heavy fire which caused some loss and killed Captain Kirk of the grenadiers. Captain Kilpatrick at once put himself at the head of the grenadiers, desiring them, if they loved their captain, to follow him and avenge his death, when, as Lawrence afterwards wrote describing the action, ' the fellows roused in an instant, swore after their manner they would follow him to hell,' and avenge Kirk's death.

The French broke without awaiting the shock, and ran off to Weycondah galled by Dalton's guns, leaving three field-pieces in Lawrence's hands.

Brenier now moved up his main body, but his men seeing Lawrence's full force in motion lost heart, and without firing a shot ran off in confusion to the Five Rocks. The Tanjore horse, who might have destroyed them, refused to pursue, and so ended the second battle of the Golden Rock.

Lawrence marched into the city with his convoy and the captured guns. One hundred French soldiers were killed and wounded ; of the English, about forty, principally by artillery fire.

A fortnight later Lawrence moved out against Weycondah, where Brenier had thrown up entrenchments. The French abandoned the position without resistance and took post at Mootoochellanoor on the Cauvery west of the city, leaving a gun and some baggage in Lawrence's hands.

Here Brenier was joined by strong reinforcements under M. Astruc, consisting of 400 French, 2,000 sepoys, six guns, and 3,000 Mahratta cavalry, together with a great number of irregular infantry.

The English were again outnumbered, as they had ever been. Astruc assumed command, and reoccupying the Five Rocks and the Golden and Sugar Loaf Rocks, entrenched himself and recommenced the blockade.

Lawrence moved out into the open south-east of the French Rock, to assist the convoys from Tanjore while awaiting a reinforcement on its way to him. For eighteen days the two armies remained encamped at two miles' distance apart on the open plain. On the night of the 18th September Lawrence seized a small eminence and with an 18-pounder opened fire on the French camp.

The French detached a party against the 18-pounder ; a skirmish ensued, under cover of which the expected reinforcements, consisting of 237 men of the corps and 300 sepoys under Captain Ridge, joined without molestation.

With Ridge also came Captain Caillaud, destined in time to succeed Lawrence as Commander-in-Chief, and who, among other performances, outwitted D'Auteuil on this very ground four years later.

Lawrence at once took the offensive ; his troops were in high spirits, but he had only three days' provisions, so prompt action was necessary.   Depositing his tents in the city he drew up his little army at the Fakeers Tope at daybreak on the 20th September, and offered battle.

M. Astruc not accepting the challenge, the cannonade from the 18-pounder was maintained, and after dark preparations were made for attack.   Lawrence's force consisted of 600 men of the corps in three divisions, 100 English artillerymen with six guns, 2,000 sepoys, and the Tanjore cavalry and matchlockmen.

At four o'clock on the morning of the 21st September the army started, the corps marching in three divisions in column, the guns were disposed on either flank, and the sepoys followed in two lines in rear of the guns, the Tanjore cavalry in rear of the whole.   The object of the first attack was the Golden Rock, on which Astruc had posted 100 Frenchmen, 600 sepoys, and two guns, with two companies of topasses.

There was a bright moonlight, but clouds obscured the moon as the force moved out, so that they reached the Rock before they were discovered.   Pouring in a volley the corps rushed to the assault with such ardour that the enemy fled precipitately, without even waiting to fire their two guns which were loaded with grape.

Without halting the force again advanced, the corps in line, with the sepoys in short echelon on either flank. Lawrence's plan was to penetrate the native camp and through it to attack the French, thus turning the latter's entrenchment, while the Tanjore horse were directed to move against the French front and threaten an attack in that quarter.

With drums beating, portfires lighted, and the sepoys' native instruments in full blast, the British force advanced

with loud cheers into the Mysore camp, spreading consternation everywhere. Nine French guns were brought into
action, but with such ill effect in the dark that they mostly
harmed their native allies. The English sepoys kept up a
brisk fire, while the corps marched with fixed bayonets at
the ' shoulder.'

As day was breaking the Mysore camp was cleared
and the French battalion was discovered drawn up in line
with a large body of sepoys on their left flank, while another
large body had taken post on the Sugar Loaf Rock. Reserving their fire as they advanced, the English battalion
was received with a volley at twenty paces, which caused
considerable loss : Captain Kilpatrick, leading the grenadiers, falling desperately wounded. The sepoys, however,
on the left of the French line broke and fled under the fire
of the English sepoys, and Caillaud, who had taken Kilpatrick's place, seized the opportunity and wheeled up
the right division of the corps on the uncovered flank of
the French battalion, and then pouring in a heavy fire
charged with the bayonet, rolling them up on their centre,
while the remainder of the corps fell upon them in
front.

The French then fell back in disorder, Astruc doing his
best to rally them, but the grenadiers were on them again
before they could reform, and in a moment the whole
French force dissolved and fled in complete derangement.

The English sepoys on the left, who had taken no part
in the engagement so far, pushed on to the Sugar Loaf
Rock, which they carried, defeating and dispersing the
French sepoys posted there.

The whole action, known as the ' Battle of the Sugar
Loaf Rock,' scarcely lasted two hours ; the plain was
covered with the flying enemy, computed at 30,000 footmen
and 16,000 horse. In wild confusion the fugitives ran

without stopping till they had crossed the Cauvery and reached the island of Seringham.

M. Astruc, with nine officers and 100 Frenchmen, eleven pieces of cannon, and all the tents, baggage, and ammunition of the French camp, remained in the hands of the victors.

Dalton, sallying out from the city, took twenty-one French prisoners, sixty-five more were found straggling in Tanjore territory, and a number were killed by the country people; 200 of them were killed or wounded in the engagement, and the Mahratta horse alone, by their misconduct, saved the French European infantry from total destruction. A thousand of the French native allies were killed or wounded.

Of the English, six officers and seventy men were killed or wounded, amongst the latter being Lawrence himself. Kilpatrick, in spite of being shot through the body and receiving several sabre wounds as he lay on the ground, survived to fight again.

The action was decided entirely by the infantry; the English guns were never engaged, while the French guns were so badly served that they only inflicted damage on their own allies.

Lawrence followed up this victory by laying siege to Weycondah the same evening.

Early on the 23rd September the English sepoys, seeing some of the garrison trying to escape, made for the gateway, when a serjeant of the Madras European Regiment, a ' resolute Englishman ' whose name has not been preserved, having mounted on to a sepoy's shoulders, scaled the wall and planted the colours of one of the sepoy companies on it ; he was soon joined by others, and in a few minutes the fort was taken and nearly all the garrison killed.

CHAPTER VIII

THE monsoon setting in, Lawrence left 150 men of the corps to augment the garrison of Trichinopoly under Kilpatrick (Dalton being absent on account of ill-health), **1753** and marched with the rest of his force into cantonments at Coiladdy, fifteen miles east of the city; a small garrison was also placed in the fort of Elmiseram to keep open communications.

The corps was very sickly at Coiladdy : six officers and a great many of the soldiers died in less than six weeks. In November a French reinforcement of 300 Europeans and 1,200 sepoys, under M. Maissin, reached Seringham.

At three o'clock on the morning of the 28th November a determined attempt was made to surprise Trichinopoly, but failed. On the 1st December a chosen body of 600 French soldiers, led by an English deserter, crossed the ditch and seized a detached battery (known to this day as ' Dalton's battery ') without alarming the main garrison. Nothing more was now needed for success but to blow in a small side gate.

Elated by their first success the French disobeyed their orders and commenced firing. The alarm was given ; Kilpatrick was confined to his bed by wounds, but his orders to his subaltern, Lieutenant Harrison of the corps, were coolly obeyed. The picket and reserve hastened to the ramparts and opened fire. By great good luck the enemy's guide and both powder bearers were killed. The French, between the outer and inner walls unable to advance or retreat, were exposed to a merciless fire, and as soon as daylight appeared were glad to surrender. A number attempted the dangerous expedient of leaping down into the ditch, but few escaped without serious injury.

Eight officers and 364 men were taken prisoners, one officer and twenty-four French soldiers were killed, besides many wounded; thus 'French petulance,' as Lawrence termed it, saved Trichinopoly from the greatest risk it had run during the war.

Shortly after this Lieutenant Harrison died; he was an officer of great promise and much respected. The acute phase of the struggle was now at an end; Dupleix, at the end of his resources, attempted to come to an arrangement, hoping to win by diplomacy what he had failed to win by force.

In December news was received of the presentation to Clive, who was in England, of a 'Sword of Honour' worth £500, by the Court of Directors.

While negotiations were pending, Lawrence was encamped at Trichinopoly confronting the French troops stationed in the island of Seringham under M. de Mainville; supplies were scarce, and Lawrence was dependent for provisions on Tanjore, which involved the constant employment of convoys.

1754 In the middle of February a more important convoy than usual was on its way from Tricatopoly. To meet and escort it in Lawrence sent out a detachment consisting of 100 grenadiers and 80 battalion company men of the corps, about 500 sepoys, and four guns, under Captain Grenville, who had orders to keep his force together and if attacked to take up a position and defend himself until Lawrence could come to his relief.

M. de Mainville had notice of the convoy, and detached

THE ROCK OF TRICHINOPOLY.

(From a painting by F. S. Ward, now in the India Office.)

400 Europeans, 6,000 sepoys, and 8,000 Mahratta horse, with seven guns, to intercept it.

On the morning of the 15th February Grenville with the convoy had reached a point between Elmiseram and the river, when he was attacked. Disregarding his orders he had distributed his men on both sides of the convoy, along its whole length of nearly three miles. On seeing the enemy he made no attempt to get his men together, or to take up a position of defence, and the whole detachment was consequently overwhelmed by the Mahratta cavalry, almost without striking a blow.

The French only came up in time to save a few of them ; men, guns, supplies, and £7,000 in money were lost, and Grenville paid for his error with his life. Here, also, Lawrence lost that splendid grenadier company he had formed with such care and had so often led to victory, and which had rendered more sterling service to the State than the same number of troops belonging to any nation in any part of the world.

Of the 230 British soldiers lost on that day, only 30 men were uninjured, 100 were desperately wounded, and 50 were killed ; of the eight officers present, five were killed and the rest wounded.

On the report of this disastrous intelligence reaching Madras, 180 men of the corps under Captain Pegou were sent by sea to Devi Cottah, where they were ordered to halt until joined by some cavalry. On the 12th May a party under Captain Caillaud, of 120 of the corps, two field-pieces, and 500 sepoys, marched in the morning beyond the Sugar Loaf Rock to escort into camp a convoy of provisions from the Tondiman's country. On arriving at this ground Caillaud found it occupied by the enemy ; he at once formed line with the corps on the left, and the sepoys on the right, and directed the officer commanding the latter to attack the enemy's left whilst he advanced against the right of their position. Both attacks were made simultaneously with the utmost vigour, and the enemy were driven out of their post with much loss. At dawn the enemy, who numbered 250 Europeans with four guns, 1,000 sepoys, and 4,000 Mysore horse, made an effort to recover their lost ground, their entire army at the same time crossing over from Seringham to the support.

Captain Palier immediately marched from Trichinopoly with the rest of the British force to assist Caillaud, and reached the Sugar Loaf Rock, where the army of the enemy, amounting to 700 French infantry, 50 French dragoons, 5,000 sepoys, and 10,000 native horse, was drawn up to oppose him.

The corps had only 360 men in the field, besides 1,500 sepoys and 12 English troopers. Palier took up a position of great strength near his own camp, not, however, without the loss of several men killed and wounded, himself amongst the latter, which obliged him to hand over command to Caillaud; the French meanwhile advanced to the attack, but were thrown into slight confusion by the fire from the English guns.

Perceiving this, Caillaud ordered the ' charge ' and drove them back out of reach of gunshot, no inducement of their officers availing for a second advance to the attack. Their sepoys and cavalry seeing the flight of their European allies also retired, and all retreated together back to Seringham with a loss of 200 French soldiers and 3,000 sepoys killed and wounded; that of the English being 59 of the corps killed and wounded, six out of nine officers wounded, and 150 sepoys killed and wounded.

The detachment then brought up the convoy and quietly regained their camp. In July Lawrence marched to Tanjore, where Pegou with his reinforcement joined him.

On the 23rd July he was joined by two companies of the Bombay European Regiment (our present second battalion), which had come round by sea, and in addition by 80 men of the corps, and 200 topasses from Madras, and on the 15th August the united forces were reviewed before the King of Tanjore. The English consisted of 1,000 men in battalion, 200 topasses, 3,000 sepoys, and 14 guns, also the Tanjorean army of 2,500 cavalry and 3,000 infantry, mostly armed with muskets.

On the 16th August Lawrence and his allies encamped six miles west of Elmiseram, and M. Maissin moved from the Five Rocks to intercept him; his force consisted of 900 French soldiers, 400 topasses, a number of sepoys, eight guns, and 10,000 Mysore horse, under Hyder Ali.

Marching on the 17th August, Lawrence seized a deep watercourse and high bank between the French Rock and Elmiseram, which Maissin had designedly failed to occupy. In concert with Hyder Ali he had arranged to draw the English towards the Five Rocks, when Hyder was to seize a favourable opportunity to fall on the baggage and convoy. The plan nearly succeeded.

Lawrence, seeing the French drawn up in order of battle on his left, at once accepted the challenge and advanced in two lines. A hot cannonade ensued in which the French suffered a good deal, and as the opposing lines were on the point of commencing musketry fire, the French went about and retreated in good order to the Five Rocks.

Lawrence was preparing to follow, when he received news of Hyder Ali's attack on his rear. In his impatience Hyder had moved too soon, and was driven off when near the French Rock, but he contrived to capture thirty-five cartloads of arms, ammunition, and baggage. A separate attack made by the French from Seringham was met by a sortie from Trichinopoly by Kilpatrick, who drove them back without loss to himself. M. Maissin offered no further resistance, and Lawrence entered Trichinopoly with the loss of one officer (Captain Pegou) and eighteen men killed. The French had 160 Europeans killed and wounded. This action is known as the ' Battle of the French and Sugar Loaf Rocks.'

In September the first king's regiment sent to India since the year 1662, when our present second battalion landed, arrived at Madras; this corps, 700 strong, was known as 'Adlercron's' or the 39th Foot ('Primus in Indis'), and at the same time 40 men of the Royal Artillery, and a draft of 200 recruits for the corps, were also landed.

The French, also, at this time had received a reinforcement of 1,200 soldiers from Europe, of whom 600 were a regiment of hussars ; each side was thus able to bring into the field about 2,000 Europeans.

In October Lawrence was notified of the grant to him of a ' Sword of Honour ' of the value of £750 by the Court of Directors of the East India Company, and that King George II had bestowed upon him the rank of Lieutenant-Colonel in the East Indies.

Since its formation into a regular regiment in 1748, the Madras European Regiment, with the Bombay European Regiment, had been the only British troops in India until the arrival of the 39th Regiment, and both had been engaged and borne the principal share in all the numerous actions fought in Southern India. The devotion and gallantry of both regiments had invariably been conspicuous, and there are few instances on record where so many distinguished services have been performed by such a handful of men, with such uniform determination and valour, under peculiarly disadvantageous circumstances and against superior numbers. It is not too much to assert that the early services of these two Company's regiments laid the foundation of British power in Southern India.

During the eight years' operations against the French, in which both corps were engaged, nearly 2,000 French soldiers had been killed in action, upwards of 2,000 were taken prisoners of war (of these 62 were officers), and 105 guns were captured.

1755 When in January 1755 peace was proclaimed, there were 900 French soldiers prisoners of war with the British, whereas only 250 of the two corps were in the enemy's prisons.

CHAPTER IX

O N the 11th January peace was concluded between the French and English in India, but during the whole of the year the corps was actively employed in a harrowing and cruel campaign, bringing into sub-**1755** jection to the Nawab Wallajah his revolted subjects the Poligar chiefs in Madura and Tinnevelly. This was an entirely jungle warfare.

In October Clive arrived at Bombay from England, bringing with him 300 recruits for the Company's service; and after he landed it was decided to attack the pirate Angria's forts on the western coast of India.

On the 11th February the fleet, under **1756** Admiral Watson, having on board 800 English soldiers, the greater part composed of men of the Bombay European Regiment, and 1,000 sepoys, all under Clive, arrived off the famous fort of Gheira. After a severe cannonade from the ships the troops were landed and the fort was captured. In it was found 200 pieces of cannon and quantities of ammunition, together with naval and military stores; the money and effects of other kinds amounted to upwards of £120,000. The fleet subsequently returned to Bombay, and at the end of April sailed for Madras with Clive and many of the soldiers who had fought at Gheira, arriving on the 12th May.

Clive had been made Governor of Fort St. David, and he proceeded to take charge on the 20th June, the very day on which the Nawab of Bengal, Suraj-oo-Dowla, took Calcutta; intelligence of which event, together with details of the ' Black Hole ' disaster, reached Madras on the 16th August.

On Lawrence's recommendation Clive was offered the command of the expedition for the retaking of Calcutta : the former being too broken from age and fatigue to undertake so arduous a duty.

Advices having been received from England that war with France would shortly be declared it was decided to dispatch a force sufficient, not only to retake Calcutta, but to attack the Nawab of Bengal in his capital at Moorshedabad.

In August a sloop of war had been sent on in advance to Fulta, a town on the Hoogly below Calcutta, with Major Kilpatrick and 100 men of the corps on board for the purpose of reassuring the English refugees who had taken shelter there; and on the 16th October Clive sailed for Calcutta with 250 men of the 39th Regiment, 650 picked men of the Madras European Regiment, and 1,500 sepoys ; the fleet consisting of six ships of war and several transports, under Admiral Watson.

On the 20th December the fleet, with the exception of one man-of-war, arrived, and found Major Kilpatrick at Fulta with only fifty of his men fit for duty owing to sickness, but with seventy volunteers and subsequent dismissals from hospital his force was made up to 150 men. On the 27th December the ships weighed and reached Mayapore, ten miles from the fort of Budge-Budge, which was attacked next day, on the morning of which 500 of the corps, with 1,500 sepoys and two field-pieces, were landed under Clive, and proceeded to the attack.

After a long march, the men dragging the guns through the mud, a halt was called for rest, when suddenly the force was attacked by 2,000 of the enemy's foot and 1,500 horse, who were repulsed with considerable loss, several of the corps being wounded, and one officer (an ensign) killed. The following day the fort was evacuated, but in a skirmish with the retreating enemy Captain Campbell of the corps was killed.

1757   On the 1st January the fleet arrived before Alighur, which had been abandoned, but fifty guns were captured. On the 2nd January Clive landed with most of his force and marched towards Calcutta, the fleet having arrived before him and taken possession of the fort (which the Nawab's troops had evacuated), when the English colours were hoisted by Captain, afterwards Sir Eyre Coote, who had landed with 120 men of the 39th Regiment.

On the 12th January the fort of Hoogly was captured by a small party of men of both the 39th and the corps, under Captain Coote. News having by this time arrived of war between England and France, and there being 300 Frenchmen and a train of artillery at the French settlement of Chandanagore, it was determined to treat with the Nawab and thus prevent the junction of the French with him; but the attempt failed, and the Nawab advanced to retake Calcutta.

On the 2nd February his army entered the Company's limits and closely invested Calcutta. On the 4th February Clive determined to attack his camp; at midnight, 600 sailors having been landed, a force consisting of 650 of the corps, 100 gunners, 800 sepoys, six field-pieces, and the sailors, marched out of the fort, and at daylight came upon the enemy's advanced guard, which they at once drove in. A dense fog coming on, Clive advanced to where the Nawab was supposed to have encamped, and having repulsed a charge by a body of Persian cavalry he marched through the enemy's camp and then returned to Calcutta by another route than the one from which he had started.

It was an exhausting day's work and the loss was considerable : 27 of the corps, 12 bluejackets, and 18 sepoys were killed ; 70 of the corps, 12 bluejackets, and 35 sepoys were wounded ; Captains Pye and Bridges of the corps were killed, also Mr. Belcher, Clive's secretary ; and a civilian volunteer, Mr. Ellis, lost his leg by a round shot. The enemy's loss was still more severe : 22 officers of distinction, 600 men, 500 horses, four elephants, and several camels were killed and wounded ; and the Nawab was so impressed with dread of his enemies that on the following day he made terms, and withdrew from British territory.

Meanwhile the ship of war that had been missing arrived with the remainder of the detachment of Adlercron's regiment (the 39th),* also from Bombay two companies of the Bombay European Regiment, 400 strong, under Captains Bucannon and Armstrong, and a battery of Bombay artillery ; it was therefore resolved to attack the French settlement of Chandanagore. The ship, however, containing the detachment of Adlercron's regiment, having a great number of sick on board, was compelled to leave the river and proceed to Vizagapatam and thence to Madras, at both of which places many were landed belonging to the 39th and to the corps : so that at the very commencement of the campaign the army was deprived of the services of a number of good soldiers.

On the 22nd March the batteries against Chandanagore were completed, and next day at sunrise the ships commenced the bombardment ; the batteries on shore at the same time opened fire, and a furious cannonade was kept up until 9 o'clock A.M., when a flag of truce was hoisted, and at 3 P.M. the fort capitulated.

On shore 40 English soldiers were killed and wounded,

* And a portion of the corps.

of whom 20 belonged to the corps. On board the ships 32 were killed and 120 wounded. The enemy's losses were 40 killed and 70 wounded. Before the surrender, 50 Frenchmen and several officers left for Patna. The plunder was estimated at £100,000.

On the 19th May treaties were made with Meer Jaffier, the Nawab's commander-in-chief, to dethrone Suraj-oo-Dowla.

On the 12th June the troops at Calcutta with 150 bluejackets proceeded to join the remainder of the forces stationed at Chandanagore, and it was then decided to attack the Nawab; consequently, leaving 100 men at Chandanagore, the remainder of the force with the guns were placed in boats, 200 of which were rowed up the river, the sepoys marching along the banks.

On the 16th June the army landed at Paltee, and Major Coote with 200 men, partly of the 39th Regiment and partly of the Madras and Bombay Regiments, together with 500 sepoys, was sent to take the fort of Cutwah, which the enemy evacuated after a slight resistance; the same evening the main body arrived and encamped near that fort. On the 22nd it crossed the river before sunset, again moved, and after a fatiguing march through a whole night's rain, the soldiers being up to their middles in mud, it reached Plassey at one o'clock on the morning of the 23rd June.

Information was shortly brought to Clive that the enemy were encamped within two miles. The advance guard of 200 Europeans, 300 sepoys, and two guns had been posted in a small hunting house of the Nawab's, and had thrown out pickets in front of a grove of trees which extended 800 yards north and south, and was 300 yards broad, surrounded by a slight bank and ditch. The Nawab's hunting house was in front of it and close to the river-side, about fifty yards distant from the grove.

At daybreak on the 23rd June the enemy was observed

marching towards the grove of Plassey with the apparent intention of surrounding it. The handful of British viewed with wonder this numerous and imposing army of at least 50,000 foot, 18,000 horse, and 50 pieces of artillery, slowly advancing towards them; their guns were chiefly 18-, 24-, and 32-pounders, and each of these with its carriage and tumbril was mounted on a large wooden stage raised on wheels about six feet from the ground, and conveying, also, the artillerymen.

These machines were each drawn by forty or fifty yoke of large white bullocks, and behind each gun walked an elephant, trained to assist by shoving with his head when required to do so. A party of forty Frenchmen, under an officer named Sinfray, manned four French field-pieces which were attached to this army.

On the advance of the enemy Clive formed his force outside the bank surrounding the grove. It consisted of four divisions of British infantry : the first, under Major Kilpatrick, was composed of 300 men of the corps ; the second, under Major Grant, of 200 of the corps and 30 of the Bengal Europeans ; the third, under Major Eyre Coote, of 170 of the 39th Regiment ; and the fourth, under Major Gauh, of 200 of the Bombay European Regiment. The sepoys were formed on each wing ; three field-pieces were on each flank of the Europeans, and these and the two guns with the advance guard were manned by 100 British gunners and 50 bluejackets ; in all, the British had not more than 1,020 Europeans and 2,100 sepoys in the ranks.

The enemy, with their guns dispersed in brigades between the divisions of their troops, which were formed in deep masses, advanced slowly and attempted to surround the grove, which, however, the river and the occupation of the Nawab's hunting house prevented ; they then halted, and M. Sinfray with his four guns advanced in front of a body

of infantry commanded by Meer Moodeen, and at eight
o'clock A.M. began a brisk cannonade, the first shot of which
killed one grenadier and wounded another of the corps.

The British drawn up outside the grove, their left resting
on the river, and their right on the grove, remained for
some time exposed to the fire of all the enemy's artillery,
and in a few minutes having lost some twenty Europeans
and thirty sepoys killed or wounded Clive retired within the
grove under shelter of the mound, the left flank being still
covered by the Plassey hunting house, and by the river;
the enemy, much elated, pushed forward all their artillery
to within short range, while the British field-pieces, beauti-
fully served, continued a heavy fire on those of the enemy.

In this situation both armies remained until midday,
when on a shower of rain falling the enemy's fire was much
slackened; a large body of their cavalry at this time attempted to charge, but were repulsed by the field-guns,
and retired out of range. On the rain ceasing the enemy
again resumed the cannonade, which was kept up on both
sides until three o'clock P.M., when, having lost many men,
amongst others Meer Moodeen, their best general, they
retired to their camp; the Frenchman Sinfray, however,
still kept his position, but soon followed the rest.

The enemy's entrenchment was about three miles in
extent; in the centre was a mound mounting guns, and
between it and the British line were three more mounds, all
of which were fully armed. Major Kilpatrick, on Sinfray's
retirement, at once pushed forward and occupied the ground
he had vacated. Clive joining him on the spot, determined to
renew the attack, and ordered an advance of the whole line.

The British artillery kept up a galling fire on the crowds
in the enemy's camp, which threw their artillery into
confusion, killing and wounding many of their gunners,
bullocks, and elephants. At this juncture a large corps

of the enemy under Meer Jaffier, the commander-in-chief, made a demonstration from the right of their line, in such a manner, however, as made it doubtful whether they were friends or foes, but being kept at a distance by a few cannon shot they remained aloof.

The British were now ordered to storm the entrenchment in two columns : one led by Kilpatrick and headed by the Madras European Regiment, the other by Coote with the grenadiers of the 39th and Bombay European Regiments. The former stormed and captured Sinfray's guns, the other dispersed and completely routed a large body of the enemy.

Cavalry, artillery, and infantry all fled in one confused mass, throwing away their arms and all that impeded their flight; all their guns were abandoned, many of the elephants had been wounded and became unruly, and most of the gun bullocks had been either killed or wounded. Thus ended the battle of Plassey—not, perhaps, to be reckoned a great battle, as it was won mainly by treachery in the enemy's camp, but, as a victory, in its consequences the greatest ever gained.

The victory of Plassey was gained with but little loss to the British, the casualties amounting to only about 50 killed and wounded, of which the corps had 15 men killed and a few wounded ; the enemy lost 500 killed and wounded, in addition to the capture of all their guns, elephants, horses, baggage, and camp equipage.

On the 25th June the army marched to Moorshedabad, the defeated Nawab's capital, and on the 29th, Clive, escorted by 200 men of the corps and 300 sepoys, entered the city and solemnly placed Meer Jaffier on the throne.

The battle of Plassey was one of the last occasions on which a large portion of the corps was engaged under its distinguished commander, Clive : designated by the great Chatham ' a heaven-born general.'

CHAPTER X

FROM the beginning of the year part of the corps at Trichinopoly had been employed under Caillaud in assaulting the city of Madura, which was carried by storm on the 8th September. On the 12th May a large

1757 French force arrived at Seringham and several attacks were made on Trichinopoly, the garrison of which was much weakened by the absence of Caillaud in Madura, and amounted to only 150 of the corps, 15 artillerymen, and 700 sepoys, and these had in addition to their other duties to guard no less than 500 French prisoners confined in the fort.

On the 20th May the enemy attempted to escalade, but were severely repulsed, and on the 21st they failed in preventing Caillaud's detachment of 20 men of the corps and 1,200 sepoys from forcing their way through and entering the city.

On the 25th May Colonel Adlercron with his regiment, the 39th Foot, marched from Madras towards Wandewash, which he took after a slight resistance; this alarmed the French, who then withdrew from the neighbourhood of Trichinopoly, on which Colonel Adlercron returned to the Presidency.

Early on the 15th June 200 French and 500 sepoys, with two guns, marched from Pondicherry to burn and plunder Conjeveram. This large pagoda, between Madras and Arcot, was defended by two companies of British sepoys under Serjeant Lamberton of the corps, who repulsed the enemy with severe loss, and obtained a commission for his gallantry.

On the 19th June Colonel Adlercron with his corps, the 39th, augmented by a part of the Madras European Regiment, marched from St. Thomas's Mount, near Madras, towards Ootramalore, where much sickness broke out in camp : the mortality was great, men dying after less than twelve hours' illness ; but on change of ground the disease disappeared. On the advance of the English the French retired towards Wandewash, where on the 14th July the English encamped within sight of them.

The strength of the two armies was about equal : the French numbering 800 Europeans, of whom 100 were hussars, and 1,500 sepoys. Of the English there were 700 British soldiers, partly of Adlercron's and partly of the Madras European Regiment, and 2,000 sepoys. Lawrence had accompanied Adlercron as a volunteer, but having on the 16th June received a superior commission to the latter he assumed command, and marching out offered the enemy battle, which they declined, and on the 26th he retired to Conjeveram, leaving there 500 British soldiers and 1,500 sepoys as a garrison, forwarding the remainder to the different posts from which they had been withdrawn.

During the remainder of the year the portion of the corps serving in the Carnatic was employed in harassing the enemy's territories and attacking or defending posts. The French were awaiting reinforcements, and the English, from the same cause and the doubtful state of affairs in Bengal, remained almost entirely on the defensive.

Clive meanwhile was engaged in capturing and dispersing bodies of French adventurers in Bengal, and fearing from the arrival of the French squadron on the coast that Calcutta might again be attacked, he could not return to Madras the detachment of the corps originally sent, and which had since been employed at the different actions from the recapture of Calcutta until the end of 1757.

In August Adlercron's regiment was recalled to England, but most of the men and many of the officers volunteered for the service of the East India Company : those in Bengal joining the Bengal Europeans, and those in Madras the Madras European Regiment.

1758　　On the 1st May M. Lally and Count d'Estaing, with 1,000 Frenchmen and as many sepoys, arrived before Cuddalore, which being quite untenable was surrendered by the English on the 4th May, with the stipulation that the garrison should be allowed to march to Fort St. David, and that 150 French prisoners of war should proceed to any neutral port until exchanged by an equal number of English.

On the 6th May, fresh French troops having arrived at Pondicherry, they were at once marched out to reinforce those at Cuddalore, and on the 15th batteries were erected by the enemy at about 1,000 yards from the adjacent Fort St. David, which on the 16th May was closely invested.

On the 1st June an incessant fire was kept up from twenty-one guns and thirteen mortars, which, owing to want of powder in the British garrison, could not be returned with even a single gun. At noon the same day the French squadron entered the roads, when Major Palier of the corps concluded terms and the garrison surrendered as prisoners of war.

The French force before Fort St. David amounted to 2,500 Europeans and 3,000 sepoys.

In August a few men of the corps with 500 sepoys assisted the Rajah of Tanjore, and thus foiled the French in their attack on that city, which otherwise would certainly have fallen into the enemy's hands,

On the 18th August Lawrence took the field with 520 men of the corps and 1,200 sepoys from Madras, and attacking Trivatore took it by assault, as also Trinomallee.

In August, also, a detachment of 70 men of the corps, 50 Caffirs, 10 companies of sepoys, and two field-pieces, under Captain Joseph Smith of the corps (afterwards General and Commander-in-Chief in India), captured Terriore with some loss to the British, but much greater to the enemy.

In September, Clive at Calcutta, although learning of the fall of Fort St. David, determined not to send troops to Madras, but to employ all who could be spared against the French in the Northern Circars, so as to take the pressure off Fort St. George. For this purpose he put Colonel Forde, an officer who had volunteered from Adlercron's regiment, in command of 500 men of the detachment of the Madras European Regiment which had originally embarked from Madras, together with 2,000 Madras sepoys, 100 lascars, six brass field-pieces, and six 24-pounders for battering. This force embarking on six ships sailed for Vizagapatam at the end of September.

On the 14th September the 79th Foot arrived at Madras from England 900 strong under Colonel Draper. In August the French had possession of every small post in the neighbourhood of Madras excepting Chingleyput, held by a weak detachment under Lieutenant Airey; consequently, on Draper's arrival a reinforcement was sent to Airey under Captain Richard Smith, which augmented the garrison to thirty chosen men of the corps, nine companies of sepoys, and twelve gunners, with orders to defend the fort to the last.

Caillaud arrived at Madras on the 25th October with part of the garrison from Trichinopoly; and four more field-pieces, with Lascars to man them, were, in consequence, sent to Chingleyput. Lally seeing the importance of the place resolved, too late, to march against it with his entire force, and started on the 2nd November with 800 Frenchmen and some native cavalry and sepoys; but Draper and Lawrence having preceded him, he returned to Pondicherry, thus enabling an English convoy of provisions and ammunition to be safely deposited in the fort.

On the 20th October Colonel Forde arrived at Vizagapatam from Bengal, and on the 1st December came in sight of M. Conflans, the French commander, with his force drawn up in a strong position near Condore; M. Conflans had with him upwards of 500 Frenchmen, 36 pieces of cannon, some mortars, 8,000 sepoys, and 500 horse. Forde had 470 of the corps, 1,900 sepoys, six field-pieces, a howitzer, eight battering guns, and three mortars. The English ally, the Rajah of Vizagapatam, had 500 horse and 5,000 variously armed infantry, as also 40 renegade Europeans under a Mr. Bristol, an Englishman, who also managed four pieces of artillery.

On the 10th December the battle took place. The French battalion known as the 'Battalion of India' was opposed to the Madras European Regiment under Captain Adnet, which, after pouring in a volley which knocked over half of the enemy's grenadiers, rushed in to the charge; the French did not stand it, but ran, seeking shelter behind their guns, under a heavy fire from which they rallied; but nothing could withstand the corps, which moved swiftly on, capturing every gun, and driving the French before them in confusion.

The French again rallied in their entrenched camp, but being followed they again broke and fled in disorder, abandoning their camp and baggage. Six of the French officers and 80 men were killed, and six officers and 70 men made prisoners, all belonging to the 'Battalion of India'; 32 pieces of brass cannon, 50 tumbrils and other carriages, seven mortars, 3,000 draught bullocks, and all the French tents, were captured. Of the corps, Captain Adnet and 15 men were killed, and four officers and 29 men were wounded; of the sepoys on the English side, 100 men were killed and wounded. Colonel Forde arrived at the fort of Condore next morning, and found in it a large quantity of military stores.

Whilst these operations were going on in the Northern Circars, Lally and his entire force was advancing to the siege of Fort St. George. On the 8th December he marched from Vendalore to St. Thomas's Mount (twelve miles from Madras), and Lawrence, who commanded there, retired to Choultry Plain, not intending to risk an action with an overwhelmingly superior force. On the 12th the enemy approached, and Lawrence again retired leisurely into Fort St. George.

The garrison of Fort St. George consisted of 1,758 European soldiers, of whom 193 belonged to the 79th Foot, 1,193 to two battalions of the corps, which at that time consisted of three battalions, 140 gunners of the Royal Artillery, 80 gunners of the Madras artillery, 64 topasses, 84 Caffirs, and 2,220 sepoys. In addition, 150 European civilians were told off to take charge of and serve out stores.

Lally, Bussy, and d'Estaing were the French commanders, and their forces consisted of 3,000 French infantry, 2,000 French dragoons, 10,000 sepoys, and a powerful artillery.

1759 The siege lasted for sixty-three days; the English fired 26,554 rounds from their guns, 7,502 shells from mortars, and 200,000 rounds of cartridges. Thirty guns and five mortars were dismantled by the enemy's fire, and 8,000 shells were fired into the fort.

The English loss amounted to 33 officers, 559 Europeans, and 364 sepoys, killed, wounded, and prisoners.

The siege was raised on the 16th February, 1759, on the approach of reinforcements by sea. Thus came to an end the most notable siege that had yet occurred in India, and the last serious bid for an Eastern empire by the French.

CHAPTER XI

THE reinforcements from England brought up the strength of the European troops in the Madras Presidency to over 1,700 men, and the Council thought **1759** they ought to do something ; so, contrary to Lawrence's advice, they sent him towards Conjeveram, which Lally had reoccupied after retiring from the siege of Fort St. George.

But Lawrence's army was badly off for transport, and there was no money to maintain the troops in the field. The Council, consequently, were anxious to bring back their troops to Madras ; Lawrence, however, pointed out the evil effects of retiring in face of the enemy.

To advise the Council, he left the army and came to Madras ; his health by this time had completely broken down, and he made known his intention of returning to England.

In April he sailed with the resolve of never returning to India. On his arrival in England the directors granted him an annuity of £500 a year ; and in September 1760 statues were voted to Lawrence, Clive, and Admiral Pocock, ' that their eminent and signal services to the Company may be ever had in remembrance.'

After the battle of Condore Colonel Forde marched to the siege of Masulipatam ; but, meanwhile, the English army before Conjeveram, under the command of Major Brereton of the King's service and Major Caillaud of the Company's, marched towards and laid siege to Wandewash ; the French at the same time, leaving their entrenchments strongly garrisoned, advanced to Trivatore.

On hearing this Brereton left Wandewash, and on the 15th April arrived at Conjeveram and invested it ; by 8 A.M. the following morning his guns had destroyed the ravelin, when the grenadiers of the corps, led by Caillaud, rushed out and drove the defenders inside. An attack was being prepared by the officers in the ravelin, when an old gun loaded to the muzzle with musket balls was fired into them, killing eight men and wounding ten. Captains Stewart and Bannatyne, and Lieutenants Hunter and Elliot were killed, and Major Caillaud and Lieutenant Vaughan were wounded, the latter dangerously, as also were three other officers.

During this time, however, Lieutenant Airey with a small party of the corps and some sepoys had entered the pagoda on the other side, and the place was instantly carried.

Colonel Forde reached Masulipatam on the 6th March, the fort of which was situated on the bank of a branch of the Kistna, this river washing its southern face ; the other sides being surrounded by a swamp. After several days' bombardment the fort was carried by assault on the 7th April.

Forde in reply to M. Conflans' offer to surrender on terms, threatened to put everyone to the sword if further resistance was offered, on which the enemy surrendered at discretion.

The garrison of Masulipatam was composed of 700 French soldiers and 2,537 sepoys, whereas Forde's force consisted of but 500 men of the corps and 2,000 sepoys.* Captains Callender and Mallitore and 22 men of the corps were killed, and 62 were wounded. The sepoys, who behaved with great gallantry, had 50 killed and 150 wounded. The plunder was very valuable, and Masulipatam and the

* In addition there were a few gunners and 30 sailors from the Fleet.

adjacent countries were ceded to the British. No Bengal European troops were employed under Colonel Forde at either Condore or Masulipatam.

About the 15th October, 1759, Colonel Forde left Masulipatam by sea for Calcutta, and delivered over command of the garrison, 300 of the corps, and 800 sepoys, to Captain Fisher of the regiment.

On the 5th December Fisher marched with the greater part of the garrison to Coconada near Rajahmundry, and captured nearly all the Chevalier Poete's detachment of Europeans ; the Chevalier and a few men only escaping in a vessel lying at anchor off the Dutch factory at that place.

On the 25th July 500 men of the 84th Foot, or ' Coote's ' Regiment, arrived at Madras and joined the army at Conjeveram, under Brereton.

In August 300 of the corps marched against Trivatore, and on the 25th of that month Colonel Brereton marched to Wandewash; his force consisted of part of the 84th Foot, the 79th Foot, and part of the corps : in all 1,500 Europeans, 80 Caffirs, 2,500 sepoys, 100 mounted men of the corps, and 700 native cavalry, with 10 field-pieces. On the 27th the dragoons of the corps defeated a party of French hussars, taking prisoners one officer and eight men ; this skirmish took place near Trivatore, which surrendered on the approach of the main body.

The army then advanced on Wandewash, which was held by 1,600 French soldiers. An unsuccessful attack was made at midnight with a loss to the British of 12 officers and 195 soldiers killed and wounded ; of the former, two officers and 30 soldiers belonged to the corps. The enemy lost their general, M. de Mainville, and two officers killed, and upwards of 200 Frenchmen killed and wounded ; 30 prisoners were taken. Brereton then returned to Conjeveram.

On the 26th October, 600 men of the 84th Foot having

landed at Madras, Caillaud with 200 of the corps was sent to Calcutta, Clive having recommended that officer for the appointment of Commander-in-Chief of the troops in Bengal; and it was the remnant of these men who were transferred to the Bengal establishment in 1766, when Lord Clive reorganised the army of that Presidency. Sixty men of the corps were also sent to reinforce the garrison of Masulipatam.

On the 21st November Coote took command at Conjeveram, and at once dispatched Captain Preston and 200 men of the corps to Wandewash with the *matériel* for a siege, and there on the 25th he was joined by Colonel Brereton and detachments of the corps and of the 84th Foot. On the 26th the pettah was stormed and taken, and on the 29th the fort surrendered. The French lost five officers, 100 Frenchmen, and 500 sepoys taken prisoners, besides quantities of ordnance and stores.

Coote next laid siege to Carrangooly, which surrendered on the 10th December; five French were killed. Of the corps two privates were mortally wounded, as was also an officer of artillery.

On the 9th December, Lally having dispatched 600 French from Seringham to join the army in the field, Captain Joseph Smith, commanding at Trichinopoly, sent Ensigns Bridges and Hart of the corps to capture Cortallum and Totcum; this they effected, taking prisoners two officers and 38 French grenadiers, besides collecting Rs. 100,000, the revenue of the district.

On the 19th December the British army was cantoned at Cauveripauk, and Coote repaired to Madras.

On the 25th December Coote's force marched out of cantonments, and on the 29th both armies were in sight of each other, but beyond a few skirmishes nothing of importance occurred; thus ended the third year of a doubtful war in the Carnatic.

LIEUTENANT-GENERAL SIR EYRE COOTE, K.C B.

(From an oil painting in the possession of the Oriental Club, Hanover Square)

1760 On the 20th January, Coote receiving intelligence that the French were vigorously assaulting the fortress of Wandewash, which was garrisoned by 30 men of the corps and 300 sepoys, under Captain Sherlock, he at once advanced to raise the siege. The enemy's position was a strong one, and as the British on the 22nd drew up in order of battle the French beat to arms and formed up in front of their lines ; the two forces then commenced a brisk cannonade. The French hussars, 300 strong, were on the right of the ' Regiment of Lorraine ' of 400 bayonets ; in the centre came the ' Battalion of India,' 700 bayonets, and on their left was the ' Regiment of Lally,' 400 bayonets, whose left flank rested on the entrenched embankment of a dry tank in which were posted the marines of the squadron and some troops who had escaped from Captain Fisher at Coconada ; in all 300 men with four field-pieces. Three guns were placed between each of the battalions, 400 sepoys were stationed in rear of the marines, and 900 were distributed in rear of each of the French regiments ; in addition, there was an entrenchment at each extremity of the line occupied by 50 French soldiers ; the whole force amounting to 2,250 Europeans, 300 Caffirs, 6,000 native infantry, and 20 pieces of artillery, and in addition, 30 Frenchmen and 300 sepoys were maintained in the batteries before Wandewash ; there were also 3,000 Mahratta cavalry.

The British formed up in three lines, numbering (including 80 dragoons of the corps) 1,700 Europeans, 2,100 sepoys, 16 field-pieces, and 250 native cavalry. In the first line was the 84th or Coote's regiment on the left, Draper's or the 79th on the right, and two battalions of the Madras European Regiment in the centre, all without their grenadiers, and between each regiment ten pieces of artillery were placed in position.

In the second line, as a reserve, were all the grenadiers of

F

the European corps, making 300 bayonets, with two field-pieces, and on their flanks were 1,900 sepoys.

The cavalry formed the third line, the 80 dragoons of the corps being in the centre ; two companies of sepoys and two guns were on the left, a little in advance of the line and at a short distance from it.

As the British were advancing along the plain, Lally with his cavalry made a détour and attacked the left of the cavalry line, which got confused and galloped off the field, leaving the 80 dragoons of the corps to stand the charge single-handed. The guns, however, opened on the enemy and obliged them to hurry out of fire ; the native cavalry at the same time, recovering from their panic formed up, and led by the dragoons pursued the enemy to the rear of their camp.

The British line having advanced to within gunshot, a smart cannonade was commenced, the guns doing much execution on the French line, when Lally having rejoined them they advanced to the attack. Coote at the same time moved all his Europeans to meet them, leaving his sepoys and native cavalry behind. At noon both lines halted within 200 yards of each other and opened fire, when the ' Regiment of Lorraine,' breaking into column, rushed to the charge.

Coote's or the 84th, the regiment attacked, reserved its fire until the French had arrived within twenty paces, when it was delivered on both flanks of the French column, but did not stop its advance, and the two regiments were instantly mingled in a close conflict with the bayonet. In a few minutes the ground was strewed with the wounded and dead of both corps. The ' Regiment of Lorraine,' being crowded in column and furiously attacked on both flanks, gave way and ran back in disorder to camp.

The 84th being also in some confusion, was recalled from pursuit and formed up on its original position. At this time a shot striking a tumbril in the entrenched post caused an explosion, by which eighty of the French marines were blown up, and nearly all, including the Chevalier Poete, were killed.

The confusion this caused was instantly taken advantage of by Draper, who with the 79th, and led by Brereton, stormed that post, and although losing many men, drove all before them, occupied the position, and opened so hot a fire on the enemy's field-pieces that the French gunners abandoned their posts.

Marquis Bussy with the 'Regiment of Lally' endeavoured to retake the position, but his horse being shot under him, and the 79th advancing to the charge, his men ran away and left him a prisoner with an officer of Draper's regiment.

During this conflict on both flanks of the British line, the two corps of the rival East India Companies in the centre, namely, the Madras European Regiment and the 'Battalion of India,' were keeping up a heavy fire on each other. On Lally's repulse the two battalions of the corps, the 84th, and the reserve of grenadiers, were ordered to advance and storm the enemy's camp ; leaving their field-pieces behind they pushed on at the charge. The 'Battalion of India,' though joined by the marines and the two regiments of Lally and Lorraine, could not stand their ground but were forced to retire within their lines, where they were followed, again repulsed, and driven in total disorder behind their camp, when the French hussars gallantly threw themselves between them and their assailants, and thus enabled them to retire in good order towards the outskirts of Wandewash, where their men from the trenches joined them, having abandoned all their guns and ammunition, none of which they had time to destroy.

The fighting at the battle of Wandewash was almost entirely between the Europeans on either side. Twenty-two

pieces of cannon were taken, 800 of the French were killed
or wounded, 200 were counted dead on the field, 240
were taken prisoners, of whom 200 were wounded and 30
died before next morning; six of the killed and 20 of the
prisoners were officers, the principal of whom were General
de Bussy and Le Chevalier Godeville, Quartermaster-
General.

Of the ' Regiment of Lally,' Lieutenant-Colonel Murphy,
two captains, and two lieutenants; of the ' Regiment of
Lorraine,' one captain and one lieutenant; and of the ' Battalion of India,' two lieutenants and two ensigns, and Le
Chevalier de Poete, Knight of Malta (who subsequently died
of his wounds), were wounded.

The British lost 63 Europeans, officers included,
killed, and 141 wounded, several of whom died of their
wounds—amongst others the gallant Colonel Brereton.
Thirty-six of the killed and 14 of the wounded belonged
to the corps; 13 killed and 36 wounded belonged to the
79th; and 17 killed and 66 wounded to the 84th. Four
dragoons of the corps were wounded, 17 of the native
cavalry were killed, and 32 wounded, and of the sepoys
six were killed and 15 wounded.

During this year Clive returned to England on leave of
absence.

CHAPTER XII

THE joy at the victory of Wandewash diffused throughout the Presidency of Madras was equal to that felt at Calcutta on the receipt of the news of the victory at Plassey.

1760 After their defeat the enemy retired to Pondicherry, and Coote on the 28th January invested Chitapett, which surrendered the next day ; the garrison, commanded by the Chevalier de Tilly, consisted of four officers, 54 French soldiers (besides 73 who had been wounded at Wandewash and were in hospital), and 300 sepoys. Nine guns, 300 new muskets, and a large store of ammunition were captured.

On the 1st February Coote arrived before Arcot, which on the 9th surrendered ; early next morning the grenadiers of the force took possession of the gates, and the garrison, consisting of 11 officers, 247 French soldiers, and 300 sepoys, were made prisoners. Four mortars, twenty-two guns, and much ammunition and stores of all kinds were captured.

On the news of the victory of Wandewash the French at Trichinopoly evacuated the island of Seringham and marched *en route* to Pondicherry, but Captain Joseph Smith of the corps marched after them, and before they reached Utatoor captured thirty French prisoners—Ensign Horne of the corps capturing the small forts of Cortallum and Totcum, the only remaining forts occupied by the enemy.

Thus for the first time since any part of the corps garrisoned Trichinopoly was its neighbourhood entirely free from the French. After the reduction of Arcot Coote's force invested Vellore, which to spare the attack paid a tribute of Rs. 30,000. Trinomallee surrendered on the 29th February to a force under Captain Stephen Smith of the corps. On the 1st March Coote marched against the hill fort of Permacoil, situated at the top of a steep rock never before invested by Europeans ; the lower works were captured, and after an attempt to escalade the upper fort, during which Coote was wounded, the place surrendered ; the garrison were made prisoners and twenty-two guns were captured.

On the 9th March, near Pondicherry, the ' Regiment of Lorraine ' was charged with such spirit by the Company's European dragoons that they were thrown into confusion and had several men sabred ; and on the 12th March the fort of Amalparrah was taken by assault, the garrison made prisoners, and twenty-two guns were captured.

On the 28th March Karrical was invested. The bombardment was kept up until the 5th April, when the garrison surrendered ; 115 French soldiers, 72 topasses, and 250 sepoys were made prisoners, and besides small arms and stores of all sorts, 155 pieces of cannon, nine mortars, and quantities of ammunition were captured. The fort of Karrical, completely fortified after the modern fashion, and the surrounding districts, were thus transferred to the British.

On the 3rd April the fort of Villaporam, garrisoned by 1,000 native soldiers, was assaulted and captured by a small detachment under Captain Wood of the corps. On the 7th, Coote having recovered from his wound rejoined the army ; on the 8th he reconnoitred Valdore, and on the following day invested it until the 18th, when the fort surrendered, although the whole French force was marching to its relief and at the time of surrender were drawn up in position. Twenty guns were captured. Meanwhile the division which had taken Karrical marched against Chilambaram, which surrendered.

ǀ In every one of these captures part of the corps was engaged. On the night of the 10th May the French suddenly attacked Cuddalore and captured five surgeons, six warrant officers, and 70 men sick in hospital, dispersing the sepoy garrison ; and on the following night the attack was repeated, but a party of the corps having reinforced the garrison, the enemy were defeated with a loss of three officers and 32 men killed and wounded.

On the 20th May another attack on Cuddalore was made by 700 French infantry, 150 hussars, and 500 sepoys, who were repulsed with a loss of two officers killed, and upwards of 80 men killed and wounded. On the 26th three companies of Royal Artillery with their guns, comprising 178 men, arrived from England and joined the army.

On the 20th July, Coote with two battalions of the corps and a company of the Bombay European Regiment attacked the French army near Villanore ; Draper's and Coote's regiments acting in conjunction, the enemy retired on Pondicherry. On the evening of this day Villanore was assaulted and captured, the French flag hauled down and the British flag hoisted.

On the 17th August the Mysore army laid siege to Trinomallee, defended by a few men of the corps and four companies of sepoys ; the enemy stormed twice with much resolution, but were repulsed with great slaughter, and eventually abandoned their guns and retired to Thiagur.

Four hundred and twenty-two marines from the squadron having landed, Coote determined to drive the French within the boundary hedge of Pondicherry and to take the fort of Ariancopang. On the 2nd September part of a Highland regiment joined his force, and on the 4th Lally attacked the British camp ; he was repulsed and four French prisoners

were taken, one of them being M. D'Auteuil, the same
general who surrendered to Clive at Volcondah in 1752.

At this time, commissions of a senior date having arrived
from England, Colonel Monson superseded Coote, who then
returned to Madras, leaving Monson in command.   Monson
at once undertook the siege of Pondicherry, which he
1761 invested from the 2nd September until January 1761,
when it was finally captured by the British.   The
troops under Monson's command consisted of Draper's and
Coote's regiments, each 1,000 strong, 200 British marines
from the fleet, 150 of the 73rd Highlanders, 800 of the
Madras European Regiment, two companies of foreigners,
350 of the Bombay European Regiment, and 1,100 sepoys;
the latter under Major Joseph Smith of the corps.

During this long and arduous siege many severe
encounters between the French and British took place
with heavy casualties on both sides, including the loss,
owing to a wound, of Colonel Monson himself, who was succeeded in command by Colonel Eyre Coote.   On the 16th
January the whole of the grenadiers of the British occupied
the different gates of the fortress, the army having previously
captured the numerous flanking redoubts, and on the afternoon of the same day the French garrison under Lally having
surrendered, paraded in front of the citadel for Colonel
Coote's inspection ; there were but 1,100 of them, all worn
down by fatigue, famine, and disease.

On the 17th January the British flag was hoisted and
saluted with 1,000 guns—2,072 prisoners were taken and
600 guns were captured.

The British loss during the siege was 32 officers and
500 rank and file killed and wounded ; that of the enemy
considerably greater.   The fortress was razed to the ground,
and Pondicherry and its dependencies were at once handed
over to the Governor of Fort St. George.

On the 15th February the fort of Gingee was captured by Captain Stephen Smith of the corps, and on the same day the strong fort of Thiagur surrendered after a bombardment of sixty-four days by a force under Major Preston of the corps, consisting of a strong detachment of the corps, a large party of artillerymen, and a considerable body of sepoys and native horse. The enemy lost during the siege nearly 100 Frenchmen killed and wounded.

During March the French settlements of Mahé and Tellicherry were taken, in which service a detachment of the corps and a company of the Bombay European Regiment under Captain Gore of the latter corps participated. By the 5th April not a single settlement belonging to the French remained in all India. Thus, after a war of fifteen years' duration, in every action of which the corps had been engaged, during a period when it alone held the important fortress of Trichinopoly, and not only defeated every assault made upon it, but had on seven different occasions defeated the French in pitched battles on the plain within sight of the walls, and thrice taken prisoners, or utterly destroyed the entire investing force, they inflicted on their enemy a like injury to that intended for the British by the French, after the reduction of Madras in 1746.

On the 3rd October Lawrence again took his seat on the Madras Council, having returned to India in the *Fox* packet, yielding apparently to the solicitation of the directors. By this time he had so thoroughly won their confidence that his position was greatly improved. He was again made Commander-in-Chief of all the Company's forces in India ; and to ensure that he should not be superseded in the field by any colonel of king's troops, he received from King George III the commission of Major-General in the East Indies.

CHAPTER XIII

NO part of the regiment that had gone to Calcutta with Clive in 1756 had returned to Madras by the year 1761, except the detachment sent to Vizagapatam by Clive in 1758, and in October 1759, 200 of the corps accompanied Caillaud to Calcutta, whither he proceeded to take command of the forces in Bengal, which had been much weakened by the departure of the above-mentioned portion of the corps under Forde to Vizagapatam in 1758.

1759 In November 1759 Clive advanced with a small force, of which a detachment of the corps formed part, to the relief of Patna, which containing a small British garrison had been laid siege to by the French under M. Law, and the Emperor of Delhi. On his appearance the enemy retired and the Emperor withdrew from the province. For Clive's services on this occasion the Nawab of Bengal, Meer Jaffier, bestowed upon him the rank of Omrah of the Mogul Empire, together with a jaghire worth £30,000 per annum, so well known as ' Clive's Jaghire,' now forming ' Lord Clive's Fund.'

In August and October Dutch ships filled with troops arrived in the Hoogly near Fulta, with 700 Dutch soldiers and 800 Malays, to reinforce the Dutch garrison at Chinsura. The Dutch seized some English vessels and tore down the British flag at Fulta and Riapore; Clive, therefore, directed three English ships to attack the

Dutch fleet, whilst some of the troops, consisting of 240 British infantry, 80 artillerymen, and 1,200 sepoys, were so disposed as to bombard the Dutch fleet should it advance up the river, the remainder to be ready to prevent a junction with the Dutch at Chinsura.

Colonel Forde was in command of the troops, and on the 19th November he marched out towards Chandanagore, a position between Chinsura and the Dutch troops, should they land. The enemy, disregarding all remonstrance, proceeded up the river, and on the 23rd November landed their troops.

The British troops in the batteries at once reinforced Forde, who on the 24th November was suddenly attacked by the garrison of Chinsura, which, however, was soon disposed of with considerable slaughter and the loss of their guns.

On the 25th November Forde encountered the Dutch forces under Colonel Roussel on the plains of Badara. The engagement was short, sharp, and decisive ; the Dutch in less than half an hour were completely routed, with a loss of 120 Europeans and 200 Malays killed, 150 men wounded, and 350 Europeans and 200 Malays prisoners, exclusive of Colonel Roussel himself and 14 officers. The Dutch force consisted of 700 Europeans and 800 Malays. The British numbered 240 Europeans (a small detachment belonging to the corps), 80 gunners, and 800 sepoys.

Colonel Forde's skill and gallantry saved the English power in Bengal, and a few days after the victory Colonel Caillaud arrived from Madras with 200 men of the Madras European Regiment.

1760 On the 18th January Caillaud with 300 Europeans, of whom 200 belonged to the corps, 50 artillerymen, six guns, and 1,000 sepoys marched from Moorshedabad towards Patna, which was threatened by the Emperor of Delhi with 50,000 men; he relieved the garrison and fought a battle on the 23rd May (after months of manœuvring and many indecisive actions), when the enemy were defeated with much slaughter and pursued till nightfall. This action is known as the ' Battle of Patna.'

1761 In January Major Carnac succeeded Caillaud in command, and shortly after, at the head of a force, including a detachment of the corps, he attacked the Emperor of Delhi in his entrenched camp at Gyah Maunpore and completely defeated him, M. Law and his detachment of Frenchmen being taken prisoners. Another victory at Beerbhoom, where Major York commanded, entirely dispersed the Emperor's army and induced him to come to terms with the English.

1763 Meer Cossim Ali, who had succeeded Meer Jaffier as Nawab of Bengal, having rebelled against the English, Major Adams (of great Indian fame, but whose name and deeds, like those of so many others, have been forgotten) on the 2nd July, with a force of 750 British soldiers, of which the detachment of the corps formed part, 1,200 sepoys, and some native cavalry, marched against him and gained a victory near Moorshedabad on the 19th, in which the corps participated, as also on the 24th at the storming of the lines at Mootejil.

On the 2nd August the detachment of the corps shared in the victory of Gheriah, the severest action the English ever had with a native army. Cossim's troops, disciplined after the English fashion, were commanded by a Belgian renegade named Somers, or as the natives had it, Somroo, who from being a French prisoner at Trichinopoly had on his release enlisted into the corps, but soon afterwards deserted. The action lasted four hours, and few fields have been more obstinately contested.

The English line was at one time broken and two guns captured. The British were attacked both in front and rear at the same time; their firmness, however, in the end prevailed and the enemy were defeated with much slaughter, losing all their cannon and baggage.

The English force did not exceed 3,000 men, the British regiments engaged being the 84th Foot and detachments of the Madras and Bombay European Regiments and of the Bengal Europeans. The enemy numbered 8,000 foot, 30,000 cavalry, and 30 guns.

After the battle the enemy fled to a strong entrenched position on the Undwa river known as Udhanala, near to and covering Mongheer. On the 11th August the British approached the entrenchment ; the ground in front was deep and swampy, with a ditch sixty feet broad full of water, leaving only a small footpath on the bank of the river.

The British, constantly harassed by the enemy's cavalry, were kept in check until the 15th September, when after a desperate resistance the entrenchment was gallantly carried. The enemy fled, hotly pursued, to Mongheer, which had been strongly garrisoned.

Meer Cossim, however, continued his flight to Patna, carrying his English prisoners with him ; meanwhile, Mongheer had been invested, and in October surrendered.

The loss of Mongheer so enraged Cossim that he had all his European prisoners massacred ; his Belgian commander Somroo with a company of sepoys carried the barbarous order into execution. Somers, or Somroo, invited the gentlemen to a supper, and when they were entering the supper-room Mr. Ellis was seized by the hair of his head from behind, whilst some one cut his throat. Mr. Lushington being close to him knocked the murderer down, seized his sword, killed one man and wounded two more before he himself was dispatched. The rest of the party taking the

alarm defended themselves for some time with the plates
and bottles on the table, and even repulsed the sepoys, who
were unwilling to act, until Somers ordered them to mount
on the roof and fire down through it ; this they reluctantly
did, and forty-nine English gentlemen and a young child
of Mr. Ellis were slaughtered. The private soldiers were
dispatched sixty at a time ; a few of these belonged to the
corps. A Doctor Fulerton was the only person whose life
was spared.

The English then advanced against Patna and in eight
days carried it by storm, losing four officers and 40 men
killed ; the enemy lost 1,500.

After the loss of Patna Meer Cossim withdrew from the
provinces, thus ending a four months' campaign, during
which Major Adams cleared the country of the enemy,
after fighting four battles, forcing several strong entrenchments and passes, taking two strong forts, and capturing
500 pieces of cannon; and this against one of the best native
armies ever seen in India, numbering 60,000 men, with a
force of 3,000, of which 750 men only were soldiers of the
84th, the Madras and Bombay European Regiments, and of
the Bengal Europeans.

In August of this year the corps in the Carnatic marched
to Madura against Mahomed Issooff, a dependant of
Mahomed Ali, the *protégé* of the English, and formerly a
staunch brave soldier in the British service ; his capture
was effected only after much bloodshed and treasure had
been expended, and even then, by the treachery of a Frenchman in his service.

In this harassing warfare the corps suffered severely :
two officers were killed, eight wounded, and 150 rank and
file were killed and wounded; but they succeeded in the
subjugation of the Nawab and of all the country round
Madura.

1764   On the 15th October Mahomed Issooff was hanged as a rebel against Mahomed Ali, the Nawab Wallajah of the Carnatic.

On the 3rd May the detachment of the corps in Bengal was present in the action under the walls of Patna when the armies of the Emperor of Delhi and Sujah Dowla were defeated with great slaughter by Major Carnac ; they were also present with the Bombay regiment, on the 22nd October, at the battle of Buxar under Major Monroe, when after a severe action which lasted from 9 A.M. until noon the three armies of the Emperor, of Sujah Dowla, and of Cossim Ali were again routed, with a loss of 6,000 men killed and wounded and 130 pieces of cannon captured. The loss to the British was also considerable. A few days after the battle of Buxar the Emperor came over to the English army, which advanced to Benares.

1765   Sujah Dowla, having been joined by the Mahrattas, again took the field. General Carnac marched against the enemy on the 20th May, met them at Calpy, defeated them with the greatest slaughter, and entirely dispersed them. Sujah Dowla surrendered, and thus at one and the same time were the Emperor and Sujah Dowla prisoners in an English camp.

In January, on the Nizam of Hyderabad invading the Carnatic, a force under Colonel Campbell, in which were the greater part of the corps, marched against him, when the Prince quickly retreated to his own country.

In May Lord Clive landed at Calcutta from England, as Governor-General, after an absence of four and a half years from India.

1766   In 1766 a reorganisation of the Company's European troops took place in all the Presidencies, and in Bengal the remnants of the detachments of the Madras and Bombay regiments there serving were incorporated into the Bengal European regiments, which for the first time were made into administrative battalions, three in number.

1767 In January 1767 Lord Clive left India, and died in London on the 22nd November 1774.

On Clive's arrival in England, among other marks of distinction conferred upon him, he was installed a Knight of the Bath.   At the time of his death Lord Clive, Baron Plassey, was Lord Lieutenant of Montgomeryshire, Major-General in the East Indies, and representative in Parliament for the town of Shrewsbury.

CHAPTER XIV

IN April General Stringer Lawrence bade a final farewell to India. He was succeeded as Commander-in-Chief by General Caillaud, who in turn was succeeded by General Joseph Smith, both of the corps. On the 10th January 1775 Lawrence died in London, and was buried at Dunchideock near Exeter, in the church of which parish a handsome monument was erected to his memory by Sir Robert Palk, who had been Governor of Madras when Lawrence was Commander-in-Chief. Sir Robert also caused a lofty tower to be built in honour of his friend on an eminence in his private park at Haldon, close by.

1766

If the best general is he who makes the fewest mistakes Lawrence's name should occupy a high position on the list of commanders. In the field he exhibited all the qualities of a great commander. In front of the enemy his self-possession never deserted him at the most trying moments. On no occasion did he ever hesitate, or convene a council of war, as Clive did before Plassey. Never forcing a battle without necessity, he struck with all his force and with the greatest daring when the opportunity occurred. In council his judgment was as sound as it was in the field ; among prominent men of his time he stands alone in having left no trace of personal ill-feeling attached to his name. D'Auteuil, Law, De Kerjean, Astruc, Brenier, Astruc again, Maissin, Lally—every French leader who crossed swords with him retired defeated from the combat or had to yield himself a prisoner. When the expedition was being prepared to avenge the horrors of the ' Black Hole ' of Calcutta, ill-health alone prevented Lawrence from taking the command. Lawrence, and not Clive, would have triumphed at Plassey had the former's health permitted him to assume the command.

Lawrence early discovered and fully employed the talents of those under his orders, and we find him on all occasions more forward to proclaim their deeds than to blazon his own. To this quality, which is the truest test of a high and liberal spirit, England is principally indebted for all the benefits she derived from the services of Clive. Clive continued through life fully sensible of the magnitude of his obligations to Lawrence, towards whom he ever cherished the most affectionate gratitude.

Since Lawrence's day many illustrious men have contributed to the consolidation of the British Empire in India, but to Lawrence alone belongs the glory of laying the foundations of that empire by his long and brilliant successes against the French in the middle of the eighteenth century, and but for which France, and not England, would at this day be supreme in that country; and none has a better claim to be remembered than Stringer Lawrence, ' the Father of the Indian Army.'

On his death the directors of the East India Company voted a sum of £700 for the erection of a monument to his memory in Westminster Abbey in testimony of their gratitude for his eminent services.

By the Treaty of Paris of 10th February 1763 Pondicherry was given back to the French, and at the same time the Northern Circars were ceded to the British by Nizam Ali of Hyderabad in the Deccan, who having declared war in conjunction with the Mahrattas, against Hyder Ali the ruler of Mysore, the British, being allies of the former, became embroiled in it.

MONUMENT TO MAJOR-GENERAL STRINGER LAWRENCE
IN WESTMINSTER ABBEY.

1767 In May the Mahrattas invaded Mysore, whilst Nizam Ali with a detachment of the Madras army under Colonel Joseph Smith of the corps marched and joined the Mahrattas under the walls of Seringapatam.

Hyder, however, bought off the Mahrattas, and then formed an alliance with the Nizam. Colonel Smith, finding himself deserted in the vicinity of two overwhelming armies, retired into the Carnatic, his force amounting only to 800 men of the corps, 30 of whom were mounted as dragoons, 1,000 Nawab's cavalry, 5,000 sepoys, and 16 field-pieces.

The armies of the Nizam and Hyder numbered 42,000 cavalry, 28,000 infantry, and 109 guns. On the 28th August Smith marched towards Trinomallee, where he was to be joined by 400 additional men of the corps and 4,000 sepoys from Trichinopoly ; the march was harassed by clouds of the enemy's cavalry, who hung on the skirts of the column.

On the 3rd September the road led through the small pass of Changama, which the enemy's infantry were rapidly advancing to secure ; but Colonel Smith pushing on arrived before them and formed up in line of battle. A severe action ensued, the enemy making repeated charges *en masse* which were gallantly repulsed, and the enemy driven back with a loss of two guns. The British continued their advance, and after hard fighting drove their assailants in confusion before them.

The enemy in this action, called the 'Battle of Changama,' lost in killed alone upwards of 2,000 men, the British loss being 170. Colonel Smith then marched to Trinomallee.

On the 25th September Colonel Joseph Smith moved out his entire force: 1,400 Europeans, the greater number of whom belonged to the corps, 30 dragoons of the corps, 9,000 sepoys, 34 field-pieces, and 1,500 Nawab's cavalry. The enemy's camp, four miles from Trinomallee, was entrenched, and in a chain of redoubts along it numerous guns were mounted.

The British encamped out of gunshot, and at noon on the 26th the enemy moved out in force. Smith immediately advanced to the attack, but making a flank movement Hyder concluded he was retiring to Arcot ; the nature of the ground concealed the movements of the rival armies, when suddenly the advanced guards of both met. The British army was rapidly formed in line, its right resting on a hill, and its left on some rocks from which the enemy had just been driven.

Hyder's and the Nizam's armies drew up on some heights at a short distance from and parallel to the British. Smith's guns were splendidly served, and advancing with the line, had nearly silenced those of the enemy when they were turned on the masses of cavalry who threatened the British flanks. In a few minutes the rapid and well-directed fire of the Madras artillery quickly covered the field with disorganised masses of flying cavalry ; the enemy's infantry and guns, however, continued to maintain their ground.

On the continued steady advance of the British line Hyder eventually withdrew his guns, but nine of those belonging to Nizam Ali were captured by a charge of a portion of the corps.

The Nizam shortly fled from the field, but Hyder fell back and reoccupied his entrenched camp. At midnight the British stood to their arms and proceeded in silence to beat up the enemy's camp ; at daybreak they found it had been abandoned, but the road as far as the eye could reach was covered with the flying troops and their baggage, Hyder in person commanding the rear guard. The British pressed forward, and the advance guard, headed by a strong party of picked men of the corps, drove the enemy back and captured fifty-five of the Nizam's heavy brass guns. The pursuit lasted till midnight, when Colonel Smith halted his exhausted and overworked troops after nearly thirty-six hours' fighting, with a scarcity of food amounting to actual famine ; and thus ended the battle of Trinomallee.

The General marched back his starving army to Trino-mallee ; during the two days' operations his losses had amounted to 200 killed and wounded, while the enemy lost 4,000 men and 64 brass guns.

On the 7th December a force from Vellore, of which 1,000 of the corps formed part, started under Colonel Joseph Smith to the relief of Amboor, a fort situated on an almost impregnable rock which had been bravely defended for nearly a month against Hyder Ali's whole force by Captain Calvert, one other officer, a serjeant, and 15 men of the corps, together with 500 sepoys of the 10th Native Infantry. On Colonel Smith's approach the enemy raised the siege and retired.

On the 8th December Colonel Smith pursued the enemy to Vaniambaddy, where they were drawn up in a strong position ; the engagement lasted for a short time only, with but slight loss to either side. The enemy retreated, but pursuit was impossible, Hyder's transport being far superior to that of the British. During the action Hyder's troop of French cavalry deserted him, and came over to the British.

Towards the end of December the enemy's cavalry prevented convoys moving without very strong escorts, and against one in particular under Captain FitzGerald, expected to move by the Singarpetta Pass, Hyder com-manded in person, and proceeded to capture it with 4,000 cavalry, 2,000 infantry, and six guns ; but Colonel Smith suspecting his intentions, reinforced FitzGerald with two companies of grenadiers of the corps, a battalion of sepoys, and two guns, which joined unperceived by the enemy.

Hyder, unaware of the reinforcement, attacked the convoy with more spirit than prudence ; charging at the head of his cavalry on the grenadiers he nearly fell into their hands, had his horse shot under him, and a bullet went through his turban. His cavalry were severely handled and experienced a heavy loss, several of their officers, also, being killed.

The convoy reached camp in safety, and Hyder was deeply mortified at his failure. About this time a peace was concluded with the Nizam.

1768   In April Kistnagherry was blockaded by General Joseph Smith, and it surrendered on the 2nd May ; Colonel Wood's division at the same time marched into the Baramahal country, and before the end of May captured sixteen hill forts ; in all of which engagements part of the corps participated. General Smith's army at this time was concentrated at Kistnagherry for the invasion of Mysore, and on the 8th June it set out, its advance guard composed of a strong detachment of the corps, three battalions of sepoys, with artillery and cavalry, under Colonel Dugald Campbell. The army ascended the pass of Boodicotta, and on the 15th June captured the fort of Vencatagherry, as also, on the 27th, the strong forts of Mulwalgul and Colar. General Smith was at this time accompanied by Mahomed Ali, Wallajah Nawab of the Carnatic, and by two field deputies sent by the Government of Madras.

CHAPTER XV

THE invasion of Mysore by the British was commenced on the 1st July, but General Joseph Smith, the commander, was hampered and delayed by the conduct of the Madras Government, owing to which the campaign became a fiasco from beginning to end. It is true that the army gained a few victories, notably that at Arlier, and that nothing could exceed the valour and devotion of the troops, especially that of the men of the corps, but several outlying forts previously so gallantly won were recaptured by the enemy and their garrisons sent prisoners to the dungeons of Seringapatam ; and all this owing to the want of supplies and the overwhelming hordes of Mysoreans, led by Hyder Ali, the ablest Indian general of his day.

1768

The year closed with these events ; a gallant and devoted corps of Europeans, both artillery and infantry, a faithful army of well-disciplined sepoys, were frittered away and sacrificed to an inefficient and corrupt Government, and the energy and ability of General Joseph Smith, an excellent, high-spirited officer, paralysed and thwarted by those to whom he had a right to look for support and co-operation.

It was a notorious fact that when the army was put to the greatest straits for food, and frequently left to famish, there was no reason why, under proper and less infamous management, they should not have been abundantly supplied. To crown all, the Government of Madras sued for

peace, and twelve days' cessation of hostilities was granted ;
1769 but no terms having been agreed upon, hostilities were resumed on the 6th March 1769, when the whole of the Carnatic was once more in flames.

In a series of masterly movements, when General Smith from his vicinity to the Presidency was enabled to move his guns as quickly as the enemy could move theirs, Hyder was so repeatedly outmanœuvred that he became most desirous to make peace ; and whilst the rival armies were about 140 miles distant from Madras he, accompanied by 6,000 cavalry and 200 infantry, marched 130 miles in three days, and appeared on the 29th March before Madras, within five miles of Fort St. George. He sent word to the Governor that he had come to conclude terms, and requested that the senior member of Council might be sent to him. On the 2nd April the treaty was definitely settled and signed.

During this eventful war the troops had done more than could have been expected from any but British soldiers. On every occasion they had behaved with the greatest gallantry, and had not General Joseph Smith been at all times thwarted by the corrupt measures and incapacity of the Government, it would have been spared the disgrace of having a treaty dictated to it almost within gunshot of the ramparts of Fort St. George.

Hyder invariably spoke in terms of the highest praise of the talents and character of General Smith—a tribute due from one great soldier to another. General Smith's conduct throughout the war must ever secure for him the reputation of being one of the best officers of his day, for he never committed one military error in all his numerous and rapid dispositions. Of Hyder Ali it may be said that he showed himself the best Indian general of his day, and to the honour of the corps it may be asserted, that the British officer he expressed the highest opinion of, and which he made no secret of avowing, and the only officer he ever refrained from encountering, was General Joseph Smith, who had risen in the corps, and had learned his profession under Lawrence and Clive, the best masters of the science of Indian warfare.

When Hyder left St. Thomas's Mount on his return to Seringapatam, he expressed great anxiety to have an interview with his 'Preceptor,' as he styled General Smith; circumstances prevented the wish being gratified, but he then begged to have a portrait of the General, which some time afterwards was sent, and after the capture of Seringapatam in 1799 was found in the palace there and was sold as prize property. Subsequently, the General being then dead, it was sent to England, and went into possession of the late General David Smith, of Combe Row, Somersetshire.

1771 On the breaking out of hostilities with Tanjore in September 1771, a force under General Smith, of which the corps and all the grenadiers formed part, was assembled at Trichinopoly; it reached the capital of Tanjore on the 29th, and after some fighting and skirmishes with the garrison the place was invested, and by the 27th October a practicable breach was made, when the Rajah came to terms, and the force returned to Trichinopoly.

1772 On the 12th March 1772 General Smith with the corps, all the grenadiers, and a body of sepoys left Trichinopoly for the purpose of capturing Ramnad. During May the fort was stormed; the grenadiers, commanded by Captain Robert Godfrey, particularly distinguished themselves, and Lieutenant Burr (afterwards Lieutenant-General Daniel Burr), a grenadier subaltern of the corps, was one of the first to effect a footing on the breach.

The fort of Callacoil was shortly afterwards captured by Colonel Abraham Bonjour of the corps, with severe loss to the enemy.

1773   On the 6th July 1773 General Smith again commanded a force for the reduction of Tanjore, the Madras European Regiment and the grenadiers of the corps forming part of it. On the 3rd August the force marched, and by the 5th, after some sharp skirmishing, arrived within a short distance of Tanjore. The same night the grenadiers attacked the enemy's cavalry camp and completely surprised and routed them with much slaughter. On the 20th August approaches were made to within 500 yards of the city walls. On the 24th the enemy made a determined sortie, but were driven back with great loss, the grenadiers particularly distinguishing themselves.

On the 16th September the breach was practicable, and seven men of the corps volunteered to complete a passage over the wet ditch with fascines ; of these six were killed or wounded, and at 1 P.M. the same day the troops advanced to the assault, and although 20,000 men were in the fort ready to defend it to the utmost, yet they were taken by surprise and the place fell easily.

The Rajah and his family, the Prime Minister, and the Generalissimo, with many men of consequence, were taken prisoners, after which the troops marched back to Trichinopoly. During the siege about sixty of the corps were killed or wounded ; amongst the latter Colonel Fletcher, with an arrow in his mouth.

1775   Early in 1775, on the breaking out of the Mahratta war, two grenadier companies of the corps and a battalion of sepoys left Madras for service in Guzerat, and joined the Bombay force under Colonel Keating at Cambay in April. These two companies were commanded by Captains Myers and Serle of the corps.

On the 18th May, as the British and their ally were marching over the plains of Arras, their rear was fired upon by artillery posted in enclosures. The detachment of grenadiers of the Madras and Bombay European Regiments, with a strong party of sepoys, was directed to storm the guns; on their approach the enemy retired at full speed with their artillery, but threw in a large body of cavalry and elephants to cover their retreat, whilst another mass of cavalry and elephants penetrated between the rear of the grenadiers and the Bombay European Regiment, and pretended to be part of our ally Rugoba's army, their assertions being confirmed by an officer in our treacherous ally's service. In this, however, the British were deceived, and our Mahratta allies proved to be traitors.

The officer in question was heard exhorting the enemy to cut off the detachment, on which they made a most determined attack, and completely surrounded it; the brave fellows, however, gallantly repulsed them both in front and rear. The British detachment, nevertheless, was eventually driven back, and lost a field-piece in the crush of horses and elephants, but it was immediately retaken by Lieutenant Torriano at the head of the grenadiers; by which time the British line had advanced to their assistance, when the enemy were driven off the field with much slaughter.

The battle of Arras lasted for four hours, and victory was dearly purchased. Out of 15 British officers with the advanced division seven were killed and four wounded; the grenadiers lost 86 men, the sepoys 160; Captains Myers and Serle of the corps were killed, and Lieutenant Toring was wounded; he was afterwards taken prisoner in Baillie's defeat, where he was again wounded, and at last fell in a subsequent engagement.

The enemy lost upwards of 1,200 men, and many elephants and horses.

After the battle the British went into cantonments at Dhuboy.

CHAPTER XVI

IN June 1778 intelligence was received of war with France, and on the 29th of the same month the three battalions of the corps and their grenadiers were ordered to march with all expedition to Conjeveram. The corps, as above, composed part of the army under Sir Hector Monroe which on the 8th August of the same year encamped on the Red Hills near Pondicherry, the French settlement, and the following day summoned it to surrender.

1778

On the 21st August the boundary hedge was taken possession of, and on the 6th September ground was broken in front of the fortress. On the 10th August the English were victorious in a naval action fought in the offing, after which the British fleet anchored in the roads of Pondicherry.

The fortress of Pondicherry was commanded by M. Bellacombe, and the fortifications destroyed by Coote in 1761 had been thoroughly restored. On the 18th September the British batteries opened, and on the 15th October a passage was formed across the ditch. Then only did the brave Governor surrender. The garrison became prisoners of war, but the colours of the 'Battalion of India' were restored to it, in compliment to the distinguished conduct of that corps.

Throughout the siege the greatest gallantry was displayed on both sides. The Madras European Regiment lost its adjutant and 160 men, and Lieutenant James O'Hara of the corps was promoted to captain for bravery in the attack on the north-west ravelin.

1779   Early in March 1779 a force, of which the corps formed part, laid siege to the French fort of Mahé on the western coast, which surrendered on the 19th, and the British moved into Tellicherry, at that time threatened by the Nairs.

1780   In April 1780 Colonel Browne of the corps, with the Madras European Regiment, 100 of the Madras artillery, and a battalion of sepoys, embarked at Madras, and on the 14th joined Colonel Goddard near Powanghur in Guzerat.   In conjunction with Colonel Hartley's force, of which the Bombay European Regiment formed part, the strong fortress of Bassein, garrisoned by the Mahrattas, was captured on the 11th December.

On the 8th February 1781 the Madras and Bombay European Regiments led the column of attack which forced the Bhore Ghaut, and assisted in maintaining the position of Kandala against the whole Mahratta army of 70,000 men.   During the retreat on Panwell, particularly near Chouk, both regiments had the honour of being on the rear guard, which suffered severely.   At the conclusion of the war the greater number of the surviving privates of the Madras European Regiment were transferred to the Bombay Regiment.

In January 1780 it was well known to every person in India, excepting the Government of Madras, that Hyder Ali was preparing for the invasion of the Company's territories one of the most numerous and effective armies ever seen in Hindustan ; and it was only when the enemy's near approach to Madras created fears for their own safety that the Council directed the movements of troops to meet and arrest the progress of the Mysoreans.

In August a force consisting of 400 of the corps, the

73rd Highlanders, 800 sepoys, and 20 pieces of artillery was concentrated at the Mount, near Madras, where they were joined by Colonel Braithwaite with 200 more of the corps, 100 artillerymen with 10 field-pieces, four battalions of sepoys, and a regiment of native cavalry from Pondicherry.

On the 26th August Sir Hector Monroe, with Lord McLeod, Colonels Braithwaite, Fletcher, and Harper, marched from the Mount to Conjeveram; his army consisted of 1,500 European infantry, 300 artillerymen with 40 guns, 4,200 sepoys, 30 men of the corps mounted as dragoons, and a few of the Nawab's cavalry.

Hyder's army amounted to 100,000 fighting men, and 100 pieces of artillery; his infantry regiments were commanded by Frenchmen; of his cavalry two troops were French hussars; of the infantry a regiment of French soldiers 500 strong was commanded by Lally, a son or nephew of the celebrated Marquis who was defeated by Coote at Wandewash.

When Sir Hector left the Mount, Hyder raised the siege of Arcot, defended by a garrison of which 100 men of the corps formed part. On the 29th August the British arrived at Conjeveram. On the 5th September Colonel Baillie's detachment, in which were 200 men of the corps, reached Perambaucum, about fourteen miles from Conjeveram, *en route* to join Sir Hector; he having been ordered down from the Northern Circars. At this spot he was attacked by Tippoo Sultan, Hyder's son, with a select corps of 30,000 cavalry, 8,000 infantry, and 12 guns; but Baillie repulsed him with great slaughter.

In the evening Baillie sent off a request for assistance to Conjeveram, Tippoo at the same time reporting to his father that he could make no impression upon the British detachment.

Monroe's and Hyder's armies were encamped near each other at a short distance from Conjeveram. Monroe, instead of at once advancing to succour Baillie with his whole force, detached on the 8th September, under Colonel Fletcher of the corps, all the grenadiers and light troops of the 73rd Highlanders, two companies of grenadiers of the corps, ten companies of sepoy grenadiers, a company of riflemen, and nine camel loads of ammunition.

Fletcher joined Baillie the following day, on the afternoon of which the united detachments marched for Conjeveram; the enemy attempted to stop them, but were beaten back with some loss, and night setting in Baillie unfortunately decided to halt until daylight.

On the morning of the 10th the detachment again marched, and Tippoo appeared on its left flank near the village of Pallilore and commenced a cannonade which obliged the detachment to halt; the sepoy grenadiers, however, under Captains Rumley and Gowdie, were ordered to storm the guns, which they gallantly did, and were about to seize them when they were charged by a large body of cavalry, the advance guard of Hyder's army, masking his infantry and guns, all pushing on to the attack.

Suddenly fifty pieces of artillery opened a heavy fire at short range within grape-shot distance, and a desperate action ensued.   The enemy, at least 100,000 strong, attacked the British in front, flank, and rear, but were invariably repulsed; the detachment still gained ground, and formed square with the sick, wounded, and ammunition in the centre.

The enemy's cavalry having been driven back on their infantry, their right began to give way, and a rapid movement by the British centre seemed to have decided the day in Baillie's favour, when suddenly two tumbrils blew up, laid open an entire face of the British square, rendered the artillery powerless, and threw the whole into confusion. The ammunition at the same time began to fail, and the enemy pressed round on all sides. Their cavalry charged the sepoy ranks and soon completely destroyed them. The Europeans, reduced now to 400 men, had meanwhile drawn together in square and occupied a slight rising ground ; the enemy's cavalry and infantry repeatedly charged this small body of men, but were invariably repulsed with heavy loss.

After the ammunition was expended the contest was kept up with the bayonet, and no less than thirteen different charges were repelled. The enemy's artillery having been brought up close in different positions, and the infantry and cavalry preparing for another attack, Baillie finding that Sir Hector Monroe did not advance to his relief, accepted terms, and ordered his men to ground arms, which they had no sooner done than the enemy rushed in and put seven-eighths of their prisoners to the sword, and, but for the humane interposition of the French officers Lally and Pimoran, not a man would have been saved.

Of a total of 86 officers, 36 were killed or died of their wounds, and 34 were wounded ; of the English soldiers, 160 were killed, and nearly all were wounded. Almost the whole of the sepoys were taken prisoners or killed. The enemy took a savage delight in cutting and hewing at the wounded Europeans, and many were crushed to death by the elephants and horses which were being constantly paraded in triumph over the battlefield.

A few who lived for a short time died miserably after hours of protracted agony during the following night and day ; others who survived joined their comrades in captivity and experienced for years the horrors of those gloomy dungeons at Seringapatam, rendered more dreadful by the constant apprehension of assassination, which, with starvation and ill-usage, terminated the career of nine-tenths of those who became prisoners to the tyrant.

H

Hyder Ali, seated in his tent six miles from the seat of action, had the prisoners and the heads of the slain brought before him ; among the first of the former was Colonel Baillie. Hyder exulted over his captives, which Baillie returned with haughty contempt. The heads of the slain were in many cases placed before him by the English prisoners. Those of Captain Phillips of the grenadiers of the corps, and of Doctor Wilson the surgeon, were presented by one of their most intimate friends, and next morning the head of Colonel Fletcher of the corps was brought in.

Towards the end of the day a tent was pitched for the prisoners, but they were allowed neither food, straw, nor bedding ; all had been stripped of their clothing, and the wounds of none had been dressed. A French surgeon and the French officers as far as they were allowed behaved with the greatest humanity. Shortly afterwards most of the wounded prisoners were dispatched to Seringapatam, and the remainder towards Arnee. The sufferings of the soldiers, placed in bullock carts, exposed to the heat of the sun almost naked, taunted and abused by their savage and brutal captors, and dragged in triumph round any town or village they passed through, were too horrible to be described.

Very few lived through their captivity, nearly all dying of starvation and want of medical treatment, and a great many were either poisoned or barbarously murdered. A few of the officers survived, amongst others Captains Gowdie and Bowser, both of the corps, who lived to command the Madras army, and subsequently contributed towards the downfall of the tyrant and the taking of his capital.

Of the corps present at Pallilore, there were two grenadier and two battalion companies, with twenty-two officers ; of the latter, six were killed, nine were wounded, two died of their wounds, and five were made prisoners. Of the 73rd

Highlanders, three officers were killed and four wounded; among the latter was Captain, afterwards Sir David Baird.

On the following morning a wounded sepoy announced the disastrous intelligence to Sir Hector Monroe, when the latter commenced a retreat to Chingleyput, where after some severe fighting he arrived on the 12th September, with the loss of nearly all his baggage.

The British then encamped near the Marmelong bridge, near Madras, while Hyder took up a position forty miles off.

CHAPTER XVII

WHEN the intelligence of this disastrous campaign reached Calcutta, the Governor-General, Mr. Warren Hastings, lost no time in adopting energetic measures ; he at once suspended the Governor of Madras, and **1780** on the 13th October dispatched Sir Eyre Coote ' to vindicate the rights and honour of the British arms.'

This great commander left Calcutta by sea with a large treasure, a battalion of the Bengal European Regiment 350 strong, 200 gunners, and 670 lascars. Ten battalions of sepoys were at the same time sent south by land. On the 5th November Sir Eyre Coote with his reinforcements arrived at Madras, and by the 14th December all was ready and the army marched, and encamped at St. Thomas's Mount ; it consisted of the 2nd Madras Cavalry, the Tanjore grenadiers with two 18-pounders, the 2nd, 7th, 15th, and 16th Battalions of sepoys, the 73rd Highlanders, the Madras and Bengal European Regiments, and the Circar grenadiers.

On the 17th January 1781 the forces took the **1781** field. Sir Eyre Coote's army, consisting of 8,000 infantry, 800 cavalry, and 62 pieces of artillery, with abundance of stores, was the finest ever seen in India ; all were in the highest spirits, and on leaving the Mount expressed their feelings by loud and hearty cheers. On the 21st, 1,000 men detailed for the purpose took Carrangooly by storm, with a loss of 170 to the British, and 350 to the enemy ; a post of the first consequence was thus gained, together with an ample supply of provisions.

On the 22nd January the army advanced to Wande-wash, which Hyder had besieged since December 1780; the garrison consisted of sepoys only, under Lieutenant Flint and Ensign More, who had gallantly repulsed every assault of the enemy, besides making sorties and spiking the enemy's guns. General Coote's advance raised the siege.

On the 1st February, hearing of the arrival of the French fleet, the army marched to Pondicherry for the purpose of impeding the communication between the enemy and the shore. On the 5th the force encamped on the Red Hills, when Hyder's army appeared in great force, but as after much manœuvring on both sides he declined battle, Sir Eyre Coote subsequently encamped near Fort St. David, south of Pondicherry, where he remained until the 16th June, when he determined to capture Chillumbrum, a depôt of provisions for Hyder's army, or for any French force which might be able to land and take advantage of it.

On the 19th June an attempt to capture the fortress by *coup de main* failed, and the army retired to Porto Novo to prepare materials for reducing Chillumbrum by a regular siege. On the 1st July the army moved towards Cuddalore; the enemy occupied a strong position across the Cuddalore road, their right resting on rising ground, their left on sand-hills. A few hundred yards from the camp their line was covered with entrenchments.

Of the British force, the first line consisted of the 73rd Highlanders, the Madras and Bengal European Regiments, six battalions of sepoys, one troop of European cavalry, two regiments of native cavalry, and thirty guns, led by Sir Hector Monroe; the other, led by General Stewart, was composed of four regiments of sepoys and twenty-five guns.

One sepoy regiment, two regiments of native cavalry, and 300 Mahratta horse formed the baggage guard.

The British army filed off towards the right ; this movement rapidly executed turned the left of the enemy, bringing the British right on to the sea.   A small schooner anchored outside the surf brought her guns to bear along the whole extent of the position.   The first line advanced rapidly and drove before them thirty battalions of the enemy's infantry, who, after delivering one volley, fled.

At this time Hyder ordered a charge of all his cavalry on both lines and the baggage, that on the first line being directed by Hyder in person.   Nothing could have been more desperate and determined than their charge, but they were met by a storm of musketry and grape that few troops could withstand, their standard elephant was wounded and fled, and though a few rode up to the bayonets of the infantry and there fell, the mass wavered, halted, and at last fairly galloped off the field.

Want of cavalry alone prevented the British from pursuing the enemy and capturing most of his guns, if not Hyder himself, who would not believe he saw the defeat of his troops ; and at last he was only by force put on horseback and carried off the field.

The army then advanced a short distance along the road the enemy had fled by, and halted near the village of Mootypolliam.

Although no guns, standards, or prisoners were taken, the battle of Porto Novo will ever be considered a most important event ; it broke the spell caused by the defeat of Colonel Baillie, and it destroyed the terror inspired by the name of Hyder.   The force which gained this important victory consisted of 8,476 men, whilst that of the enemy numbered 80,000.   The British loss was 587 killed and wounded, of whom seventeen were officers.   The lowest

MAJOR-GENERAL SIR THOMAS MUNRO, K.C.B.

Joined Regiment in 1780.

(From an oil painting by Reinagle, in the possession of the Oriental Club, Hanover Square.)

estimate of Hyder's loss in killed and wounded was 10,000.

In July a detachment under Tippoo Sultan was besieging Wandewash ; Sir Eyre Coote moved to its relief. On the 18th Tippoo, after being repulsed in an attempt to storm, raised the siege. The army arrived on the 20th, and Sir Eyre Coote, after complimenting its gallant defender Captain Flint, reported to the Government that ' Wandewash is safe, being the third time in my life I have had the honour to relieve it.'

On the 2nd August Coote effected a junction with ten battalions of Bengal sepoys under Colonel Pearce at Pulicat, but before the army could move to the relief of Vellore and Arcot, it was necessary to take Tripasore, garrisoned by 1,500 men.

On the 19th August the army arrived before it ; by the 22nd a breach was effected, and orders were instantly given to storm, when the enemy surrendered at discretion.

Sir Eyre Coote now proposed to Hyder Ali to exchange prisoners taken at Tripasore, which the latter refused, and recommended the General to put all his to death !

The enemy were now encamped on the same ground at Pallilore on which Colonel Baillie's detachment was cut up in September of the previous year. Hyder determined to offer battle on the same spot and day of year, his astrologers having prognosticated a favourable issue therefrom.

On the morning of the 27th August the army marched at 8 A.M., and discovered the enemy drawn up in order of battle. The first line, under Sir Hector Monroe, advanced under a fire from eight or ten guns ; the second line, under General Stewart, formed at right angles to the first. The first line then pushed on to capture the guns under a heavy cannonade from both flanks ; the second line, also, was hard pressed, when Monroe formed up on its right, which movement brought them to the same ground where Baillie had made his last stand.

The fragments of bones, legs, arms, and skulls of their slaughtered comrades strewed over the position brought the bloody tragedy of last September vividly to the minds of the soldiers, and excited feelings of the most deadly vengeance against the enemy.

The broken nature of the ground rendered it difficult to advance with celerity, and Hyder's troops were strongly entrenched. As the British, however, approached, Hyder withdrew his guns and before nightfall his army retired some distance, leaving the British masters of the field after an uninterrupted action of eight hours' duration. During the night the enemy fell back still further.

The result of this almost drawn action added to the depression of the enemy's spirits. The English loss, however, was very heavy, that of the enemy something less than 2,000 men. Six hundred of the British were killed or wounded, almost all of the latter desperately. Colonel Browne of the corps only survived his wound until next day.

On the 29th August the army fell back for provisions to Tripasore, and on the 22nd October the force advanced on Vellore to the relief of Colonel Lang. Hyder was encamped in a strong position at the pass of Sholinghur; about noon on the 27th the British had arrived in front of his position. As the line advanced it was received with a heavy fire from seventy pieces of artillery, but continued steadily forward through broken ground, when the whole of Hyder's cavalry made a furious charge in two large bodies; one against the front of the line was severely handled and driven back, the other penetrated through openings in the line, but its flanks being protected by the rear rank facing about, they also were repulsed with heavy loss.

The British infantry with their guns then rapidly advanced, firing grape among the confused masses in their front; the right brigade at the same time gained the enemy's left flank, and its fire completed the defeat. The pursuit was continued until dark, and it was midnight before the troops were all collected on the field of battle.

The trophies were three standards, and one of Baillie's guns. The strength of the army on this occasion was 11,500 men, and their loss only 100 killed and wounded. Hyder's army numbered 60,000 men and 70 guns; their loss exceeded 5,000 men.

Want of supplies prevented the General from following up the enemy. Meanwhile, the garrison of Vellore was in sore distress for provisions; it became, therefore, a necessity either to throw in a supply, or to advance and cover the escape of the defenders.

On the 3rd November Sir Eyre Coote advanced, by rapid marches, so close to Vellore as to introduce this seasonable supply; Hyder on his approach raised the siege.

At this time part of the garrison of Vellore consisted of the head quarters of a battalion of the corps under Colonel Lang, which after the relief joined the army. Chittoor was reduced on the 23rd December, when the whole army went into cantonments near Tripasore.

Major Abington of the Bombay army, who joined Sir Eyre Coote in May 1781, dispersed and destroyed a large investing army of Mysoreans at Tellicherry, held by a portion of one battalion of the corps, with other troops, and **1782** on the 8th January 1782 marched out with three battalions of sepoys, headed by two companies of the Bombay European Regiment, and captured Hyder's general, Sudder Khan, 52 pieces of cannon, and 1,500 men.

CHAPTER XVIII

DURING the year 1781 portions of the corps had been continuously employed in all parts of India where there was an enemy to oppose them: two battalions

1781   served with Sir Eyre Coote in the Carnatic and in the defence of Vellore; one battalion served with General Goddard in the Bombay Presidency; and another, besides reducing the Tanjore country and defending its capital, and also Trichinopoly, against the armies of Hyder Ali, assisted at the capture of Nagore and Negapatam.

In 1782 the corps assisted at the third relief of Wande-

1782   wash, was present at the battle of Arnee, when the grenadiers of the corps and of the 73rd Highlanders captured a gun and eleven tumbrils, and inflicted heavy losses on the enemy, besides dispersing Lally's corps of French infantry. It also assisted in the second relief of Vellore, and early in the year Arcot and every post or fort in the Carnatic had been abandoned by Tippoo, who had been obliged to return to Mysore for the defence of his own country, then being invaded by the Bombay army from the western coast.

The absence of the Mysore army from the field of operations determined the Government of Madras to attempt the reduction of Cuddalore, strongly garrisoned

1783   by Marquis Bussy and the French army. On the 21st April 1783 the British army, composed of 1,660 English soldiers, 8,000 sepoys, and 1,000 Nawab's cavalry, commenced its march, but it was the 4th June before General Stewart reached the banks of the Panar river, five miles west of the Pondicherry boundary hedge, within which the French were entrenched.

General Stewart's force was composed as follows: H.M. 73rd, 78th, and 101st Regiments, the Madras European Regiment, Sandford's Hanoverians, 8,000 sepoys, and 1,000 native cavalry. The garrison of Cuddalore under Bussy comprised 3,000 French infantry, 3,500 Caffirs and sepoys, 2,000 cavalry, and 3,000 infantry belonging to Tippoo Sultan, Nawab of Mysore.

The British position was a strong one, its right resting on the sea, its left on the Bandapallam Hills, the ground in front covered with stunted palmyra trees and low brushwood. The grenadiers of the 73rd, 78th, 101st, the Madras European Regiment, and Hanoverians were formed into a grenadier corps, and placed under the command of the Honourable Lieutenant-Colonel Cathcart.

Early on the 13th June Colonel Kelly of the corps, with his brigade, of which the corps formed part, gained the enemy's right flank, captured a battery and turned the guns against the enemy. The Mysore troops fled, leaving an opening for the grenadier corps, the 73rd Highlanders, and a battalion of sepoys, who advanced under a severe cannonade and occupied the position abandoned by Tippoo's troops; whilst the centre attacked a large redoubt in their front. The right division also made a forward movement.

The centre attack was repulsed by the enemy, even after the 101st and Hanoverians had entered the works. The French regiment of D'Austrase left their lines and followed the retiring 101st, but Kelly's brigade on the left, with Cathcart's grenadiers and Stewart's right brigade, rapidly advanced and opened so severe a fire that the French were compelled to retire in great confusion towards their left.

When the British arrived within range of the guns on the ramparts of Cuddalore they were halted, and eventually ordered to capture the large redoubt. The bloody conflict continued until 5 p.m., when both sides lay on their arms, ready to continue the fight next day.

The enemy, however, during the night retired within the walls of Cuddalore, with the loss of 17 guns and 50 prisoners. The loss on both sides was very great : 1,030 of the British were killed and wounded, of whom 13 killed and 40 wounded belonged to the corps, not including the grenadier company, which particularly distinguished itself and lost half its number in killed or wounded. The enemy acknowledged to a loss of 850, exclusive of 14 officers killed, 25 wounded, and six prisoners.

At three o'clock on the morning of the 25th June the enemy attacked Colonels Gordon and Cathcart in the trenches, but were repulsed at all points. Amongst other troops in the trenches were the grenadiers of the corps. The enemy lost 450 men killed and wounded, and 150 were made prisoners, among the latter the Chevalier de Damas and a young French serjeant named Bernadotte, who afterwards became a marshal of the Empire under Napoleon, and subsequently King of Sweden, where his descendants still reign. The British had four officers and 70 privates killed or wounded ; Major Cotgrave of the corps was among the former.

On the 1st July a British frigate arrived in the Cuddalore Roads with intelligence of the ratification of peace with France ; hostilities in consequence immediately ceased and the siege of Cuddalore ended.

On the 2nd April 1783, previous to, and during the operations under General Stewart at Cuddalore, a battalion of the corps under Colonel Lang entered the Mysore country and took a conspicuous part in the reduction of

Caroor, where 130 men, including 60 of the corps, were killed or wounded. On the 16th April the fort of Avaracourchy was stormed and taken, and Dindigul surrendered on the 4th May. Colonel Fullerton, who had superseded Colonel Lang, captured Davapoorum on the 2nd June, when he at once marched to join General Stewart, but on arrival within three marches from Cuddalore he was reinforced by the 78th Regiment, a large detachment from the corps, and two battalions of sepoys, and ordered to proceed to Madura and Tinnevelly, for the reduction of those places, which, after thoroughly accomplishing, he again marched towards Mysore, and *en route* laid siege to Paulghaut, which was carried by the grenadiers of the force. On the 6th October a large detachment of the St. Helena regiment arrived at Madras, and was received on the strength of the corps ; these men were excellent soldiers.

1784 On the 1st March Lieutenant-Colonel Sir Henry Cosby was appointed to the first battalion of the corps, and commanded a small force, of which the grenadier company formed part, in the campaign against the Poligars of Tinnevelly. For four years peace reigned in Southern

1790 India, but on the 24th May 1790 General Meadows assumed command of the southern army near Trichinopoly, consisting of nearly 1,500 men, and on the 26th made his first march towards Mysore, the Bombay army acting on the western side.

During this year the army effected the retaking of the forts of Dindigul and others which, by orders of the Government, had been given back to the Mysoreans in 1784.

On the 2nd September 1790 General Meadows marched in search of the enemy towards the Baramahal country, where he arrived on the 10th November, but on receipt of Lord Cornwallis's orders on the 30th December, the army was directed to proceed to Madras, and on the 27th January

1791 1791, when eighteen miles from the Presidency, was joined by his lordship, who assumed command.

By the 21st February the British army, consisting of the 73rd, 75th, 77th, and the Madras European Regiment, seven sepoy battalions, and a powerful artillery, entered Mysore without opposition, and were encamped within ninety miles of Bangalore.

The army continued its march, constantly annoyed by the enemy's cavalry, and on the 4th March encamped before Bangalore. On the 6th the army changed ground to a stronger position, while the cavalry under Colonel Floyd attacked and routed that of the enemy.

On the 7th March the corps participated in the assault on the pettah gate of Bangalore, which was captured, and was also engaged in the severe action fought the same day in the streets, when the Mysore army, which attempted its recovery, was repulsed and driven out of the town with great slaughter, having lost 2,000 killed and wounded. The British loss was 131 killed and wounded, of whom 20 belonged to the corps. Among the killed was Lieutenant-Colonel Moorhouse, of the Madras artillery, one of the best officers in the army, much and universally respected and regretted.

Operations against the fortress were continued until the 21st March, during which time the besiegers were constantly threatened by the Mysore army. The infantry were invariably accoutred from sunrise to sunset, and the cavalry remained booted and saddled during those hours. On the 21st the Mysore army was drawn up on the heights towards the south-west, which would have enabled them to enfilade the trenches.

Lord Cornwallis then struck his tents, marched out and made a demonstration which obliged the enemy to withdraw his guns ; but in the evening they were again advanced, on which his lordship determined upon an assault that night. The Sultan Tippoo knew of the intended attack ; he accordingly reinforced the garrison and moved his army to within a mile and a half of the Mysore gate, and detached a force to fall on the flank of the attacking party whilst marching to the breach.

At eleven o'clock on a bright moonlight night the British advanced silently to the assault. The breach was obstinately contested, but the dash of the English soon prevailed and the ramparts were gained ; the killadar or commander of the fort was killed gallantly fighting at his post, and the flank companies of all the European regiments who composed the storming column having proceeded alternately to the right and left, scoured the ramparts, after which, meeting at the Mysore gate, they descended into the body of the place and shortly afterwards all opposition ceased.

The slaughter of the enemy was great : nearly 1,500 bodies were buried next day, but the number of the wounded was never known ; the majority fell by the bayonet. The British lost 500 men, and owing to the severity of the service many were taken into hospital. The corps lost 30 men from sickness, but being veteran soldiers it suffered less from disease than the other regiments not so well acclimatised.

After the fall of Bangalore the army marched towards Seringapatam in pursuit of the enemy. On the 13th May, nine miles east of Seringapatam, Tippoo's army was discovered in a very strong position.

Lord Cornwallis attempted by a night march to cut off the enemy from their capital, but owing to a severe thunderstorm the various regiments lost their way and the project failed ; next day, however, he offered battle, which Tippoo accepted.   The enemy were driven from position to position, but the British weakness in cavalry saved the Sultan's army, which, however, lost 8,000 men and four guns.

The British, who had 500 of all ranks killed and wounded, lay that night on the field of battle, and next day encamped out of range of the guns from the island on which Seringapatam stood.   From the loss by starvation of all the carriage cattle it was decided to destroy the battering train and retire to Bangalore.

On the 22nd May the guns were destroyed, and the army had hardly proceeded four miles when the two Mahratta armies appeared in sight, bringing abundant supplies of every kind.   Had their approach been known there would have been no destruction of the battering train, or retirement from before Seringapatam.

CHAPTER XIX

ON the 28th May the allied armies fell back a short distance, and on the 5th June marched to Bangalore, where they arrived on the 8th July. Thus ended the campaign, during which the corps had a share in every action that took place, and in all were conspicuous for their gallantry.

1791

On the 14th July Major Gowdie of the corps marched for Oossoor, which he captured without opposition, but found a large supply of gunpowder, stores, and grain in the fort. From Oossoor Gowdie's brigade marched against the strong hill fort of Rayacotta, which after some fighting surrendered ; the fort was well supplied with all military stores, together with 400 French and English muskets. After this service seven other forts were captured, with more or less resistance.

On the 14th September Gowdie's force encamped nine miles from Raymanghur. On the 16th the place was invested, and on the 17th the fort surrendered at discretion. On the 19th September the Major marched against the strong fort of Nundydroog ; his force consisted of the corps, six battalions of sepoys, six battering guns, and four mortars.

Nundydroog was reached on the 22nd September ; the pettah was stormed and the face of the rock, 2,000 feet high, reconnoitred and found to be inaccessible. On the 27th the place was invested by the army of Lord Cornwallis. After

I

the most arduous exertions batteries were erected and a gun road formed. The breaching guns could only be got up with the aid of elephants. The fort was defended by Sulf-Ali-Beg, one of the Mysore Sultan's best officers ; and after a fortnight's incessant labour two breaches were made, but the inner wall was quite uninjured.

On the 17th October Major Gowdie reported the breaches practicable, on which Lord Cornwallis detached the flank companies of H.M. 36th and 71st Regiments to assist in the assault, and at the solicitation of General Meadows sent that officer to assume command. On the 18th the grand army encamped within four miles of the rock. The grenadiers of H.M. 36th and 71st Regiments were to carry the breach in the curtain, their light companies to storm the outworks, while the flank companies of the corps, under Captain Doveton, were to escalade the inner wall.

The assault was given on the bright moonlight morning of the 19th October, and the troops had no sooner left the trenches than they were discovered ; the walls of the fortress were instantly illuminated with blue lights, and a heavy fire of cannon, musketry, and rockets opened on them, besides which large stones and fragments of rock were hurled from above on the besiegers.

Both breaches were soon carried. The flankers of the corps then forced the gate of the inner fort and were the first to enter the body of the place, which was quickly taken possession of. The garrison of 600 men were all either killed, wounded, or taken prisoners. The English lost 40 British soldiers and 80 sepoys killed and wounded ; of the former, 30 belonged to the corps.

Savendroog was carried by assault on the 21st December, and on the 23rd Ootradroog was invested and carried by storm. On both these occasions the European pioneers of the army doing duty as sappers were men of the corps, who greatly distinguished themselves.

1792 On the 1st February 1792 the British, the Nizam, and the Mahratta armies moved towards Seringapatam in three parallel columns; on the 5th the army took up a position within six miles of the city. The army of the Sultan was drawn up in a strong post covered by powerful redoubts and entrenchments; it extended from the Corrighaut Hill on the east to the boundary hedge on the west, and was composed of 5,000 cavalry, 50,000 infantry, and 400 guns, with the island of Seringapatam in their rear.

On the night of the 6th February the British stormed the Mysore lines in three columns; the right division under General Meadows attacked and carried the left of the enemy's line, Lord Cornwallis stormed the centre, and Maxwell's division entered the boundary hedge on the enemy's right and eventually joined the centre column on the island.

On the 7th the action was renewed, the enemy doing their utmost to dislodge the British from the island, but they were invariably repulsed, and night ended the battle. On the 8th February the enemy withdrew from within the boundary and were driven inside the fortress and invested on both sides, having lost 80 guns, and 4,000 men killed or wounded, besides several thousands of the troops who threw down their arms and deserted.

On the 16th February the Bombay army, consisting of four European regiments, one being our present second battalion (the Bombay European Regiment), together with seven sepoy battalions under General Abercromby, arrived and joined Lord Cornwallis.

On the 19th the Bombay army stormed and took a strong redoubt, and encamped on the heights out of gunshot. On the 23rd sixty pieces of heavy artillery with red-hot shot were in position to bombard the walls, when the Sultan sued for peace and made stipulations highly honourable and advantageous to the Company and British nation, at the same time surrendering his two sons as hostages.

At this time Major Cuppage's brigade, including a battalion of the corps and three battalions of sepoys, captured the strong posts of Damicotta and Sattimungalum, and brought up a large convoy of supplies for Lord Cornwallis's army.

1793 In July 1793, on the breaking out of war with France, a force commanded by Colonel Braithwaite of the corps, of which two battalions of the Madras European Regiment formed part, marched for the fourth time against Pondicherry, which surrendered on the 4th August ; it was garrisoned by 900 French soldiers and 1,500 militia.

1795 In July 1795 an expedition, of which two battalions of the corps formed part, sailed from Madras with Admiral Rainer's squadron for the reduction of the Dutch possessions in the Indian Ocean and the Moluccas. The land forces were commanded by General James Stewart. Trincomallee in Ceylon was besieged for three weeks, and capitulated as preparations were being made to carry it by storm.

1796 In February 1796 Colombo and Point de Galle were also taken from the Dutch, and the island of Ceylon completely subjugated, after which the corps sailed against Malacca, Amboyna, Banda, and Ternate, which were all reduced after a slight resistance.

In 1796 two small corps, one consisting of artificers and the other of pioneers, were formed from the regiment for service in Ceylon ; each corps consisted of one subaltern, two serjeants, two corporals, and twenty-six privates.

MONUMENT TO MAJOR-GENERAL SIR BARRY CLOSE, BART.,
IN ST. MARY'S CHURCH, FORT ST. GEORGE, MADRAS.

1797   On the 20th July 1797 a portion of the corps sailed for Manilla, but on reaching Penang were recalled.

1799   Throughout the siege of Seringapatam in 1799 a large detachment of the corps acted as sappers and miners.

The close of the century brings the Madras European Regiment to the one hundred and fifty-fourth year of its existence as a military body, and the fifty-second since it was formed into a battalion by Major Stringer Lawrence in 1748 ; since which time it had been forty-three years on active service in all parts of India, the greater portion of it against the French, and during that time it had in its ranks some of the most distinguished soldiers in Indian history : Lawrence, Clive, Glass, Innes, Dalton, Kirk, Yorke, Cope, Preston, Palier, Campbell, Harrison, Holt, McKenzie, Knox, Caillaud, Kilpatrick, FitzGerald, Orton, Nixon, Bonjour, Kelly, Joseph and David Smith, Stewart, Browne, and many others of earlier times, with Cosby, Lang, Gowdie, Bowser, Mackay, Braithwaite, Burr, Brown, Barry Close, Munro, and Malcolm of a later period, form a roll of illustrious names which few, if any, corps have ever produced.

During its service since 1746 the regiment or detachments from it had taken an active share in every military operation in Southern India, besides service in Bengal, Guzerat, Ceylon, and in the Moluccas. It had participated and borne a prominent and distinguished part in forty-six general actions, served at seventy-four sieges of places of the greatest importance, defended Tanjore, Fort St. David, Arcot, Vellore, Trichinopoly, Fort St. George, and Patna with the most determined resolution, captured all the Dutch islands in the Eastern seas, and been engaged in innumerable minor affairs, defences, and attacks of small forts and posts.

It was a subject of much regret to the regiment that it

did not participate in the last Mysore campaign and in the fall of Seringapatam ; but the honour of the Company's European troops was well upheld on that occasion by the Bombay European Regiment (our second battalion), whose colour was the first displayed, by the gallant Serjeant Graham of the Light Company of that corps, on the ramparts of Seringapatam, the ' forlorn hope ' being composed principally of men of that corps.

The honourable mention by Government of the names of Barry Close, Malcolm, and Agnew, officers of the Madras European Regiment, shows that they also well upheld the character of the corps they belonged to.   These officers were serving in different situations on the staff of the grand army at Seringapatam.

CHAPTER XX

O N the 13th April Colonel Burr, afterwards Lieutenant-
General, and formerly a captain in the corps, was
appointed to command the troops in the Molucca Islands,
and on the 21st November arrived at Amboyna.
1800   On the 15th December he projected the capture of
Ternate, and on the 10th February 1801 the British arma-
ment, of which the greater part was composed of the
1801   men of the corps, arrived in sight of the island of
Ternate.   The troops landed, but were unsuccessful in their
attacks upon the strong fortifications of Telooke, and
consequently re-embarked.

On the 2nd April a stronger expedition sailed from Amboyna, and arrived at Fort Orange on the 30th.   On the 8th
May nearly the whole corps landed, and after harassing and
severe service the island and its dependencies surrendered.

In 1802 the Moluccas were restored to the
1802   Dutch, and Colonel Burr brought back the remains
of the corps to Masulipatam early in 1803.   In 1802 the
flank companies of the corps were sent against the hill
rajahs of Ganjam to a place called Reddy Palarum ;
they continued on service the greater part of the year, and
in a jungle warfare in the hills lost a great number of men
from fever.

General Braithwaite of the corps died in London
1803   in August 1803.

On the breaking out of the Mahratta war in 1803 the

corps marched to Ganjam, and early in September with two Madras sepoy regiments joined the force under Colonel George Harcourt destined for the capture of Cuttack, and eventually to force the pass of Bermuth and co-operate with General Wellesley.

Juggernaut was occupied on the 18th September, and on the 10th October the town of Cuttack was given up. Immediately afterwards Colonel Harcourt prepared for the siege of the strong fort of Barrabuttee, about a mile from Cuttack. The fort was strongly built of stone, with a wet ditch varying from 35 to 135 feet in breadth, and had but one entrance with a narrow bridge leading over the ditch to it. Batteries were completed on the 13th October 500 yards from the south face of the fort, and commenced firing early the following morning. By 11 o'clock A.M. on the 14th the defences were knocked off and the guns silenced, when the storming party, consisting of a detachment of H.M. 22nd Regiment and of the corps, 400 Bengal sepoys, and the 9th and 19th Madras Native Infantry, with some artillerymen and a 6-pounder to blow open the gate, advanced to the attack; the bridge was quickly passed under a heavy fire from the fort, but it was nearly forty minutes before the wicket was sufficiently open to admit even one man at a time.

The European soldiers passed in singly and with such rapidity that notwithstanding the resistance at the inner gates they entered with the garrison, who, after a severe loss, abandoned the fort, and its capture was followed by the entire submission of the province of Cuttack.

The conduct of the storming party was gallant and firm in the extreme, and the cool intrepidity of Captain Francis Thomson of the corps was particularly remarked. Bermuth was forced on the 2nd November, the enemy escaping into Berar across the hills.

THE ROYAL DUBLIN FUSILIERS

1804 On the 17th June 1804 an order on dress was issued, when the regiment was directed to wear white pantaloons, black gaiters, hair powdered, and tail tied with a black leather thong.

1809 The corps remained at Masulipatam until 1809, during which time many recruits from England arrived and the corps was in a high state of efficiency.

In 1809 a large detachment of the corps under Captains Phillips, Forbes, and Nixon, with a detachment of artillery embarked and sailed on an expedition against the Dutch Eastern Islands.

1810 On the 15th February 1810 they landed at Amboyna. Captain Phillips attacked and carried the strong battery at Wanuitoo, killing two and mortally wounding one of the officers of the enemy, while Captain David Forbes turned the position of Battu-Guntong and forced the enemy to abandon it. In the morning batteries commanding the harbour were found abandoned, and a fire was immediately opened on Fort Victoria, which soon surrendered, when 1,500 Dutch troops marched out and grounded their arms; subsequently other posts were taken which completed the capture of Amboyna.

In August a detachment of the corps under Captain Forbes sailed for the capture of Ternate; on its landing a fort mounting fifteen guns was stormed and carried, and the following day the island surrendered. On the 29th October a detachment of the corps under Captain Nixon assisted in the attack on Banda, which also was captured.

Intelligence was received in the end of the year of the death of General Caillaud; he had retired from the service in 1775 and settled in Oxfordshire, where he lived to an advanced age, highly respected by the nobility and gentry of the county.

1811
    In 1811 the corps was under orders for Java, but the order was countermanded ; a detachment, however, served as sappers on that expedition.

1813
    In August 1813 news arrived of the death in England of Major-General Sir Barry Close, Bart. ; he joined the corps in 1772, and served throughout the early Mysore wars, became Adjutant-General of the army, and subsequently Resident at Mysore. In 1800 the Court of Directors presented him with a sword worth 300 guineas, and during the early part of 1819 erected a splendid monument to his memory in St. Mary's Church, Fort St. George, Madras.

1815
    In December 1815 the corps joined the force under Colonel Marriot before Kurnool, which place surrendered on the 15th ; the Nawab was deposed and made a State prisoner in the citadel at Bellary.

On the breaking out of the Mahratta war the corps formed part of the army of the Deccan, consisting of three divisions, the commanders being Sir Thomas Hyslop, Bart., 1st Division ; Brigadier John Doveton, 2nd Division ; and Sir John Malcolm, K.C.B., K.L.S., 3rd Division. The 1st Brigade, 1st Division, was composed of the flank companies of the Royal Scots, a wing and head quarters of the Madras European Regiment, and the 1st Battalion of the 7th Regiment of Madras Native Infantry, under Lieutenant-Colonel Thomson. The wing of the corps was commanded by Major Augustus Andrews. Five companies of the corps formed part of a brigade of the 2nd Division, commanded by Sir Augustus Floyer, K.C.B.

1817
    On the 21st December 1817 the army moved before daybreak, and had advanced about eight miles towards Mahidpore on the right bank of the Sepra river when the enemy's army was found drawn up on the other side, the intervening plain on both banks being

MAJOR-GENERAL SIR JOHN MALCOLM, K.C.B.
Joined Regiment in 1781.

(*From an oil painting by S. Lane, in the possession of the Oriental Club, Hanover Square*)

covered by the Mahratta Light Cavalry, who came forward in the most confident manner close up to the British columns.

The Mahratta army was drawn up in two lines fronting the river, the artillery and infantry in the first, their cavalry masses in the second. The village of Dooblee on the left, being the key of their position, was strongly occupied by infantry and guns and flanked by the heaviest batteries ; upwards of sixty pieces of artillery were in position along their line.

When the British had approached to within 600 yards, dispositions were made for an immediate attack. Sir John Malcolm commenced the attack by advancing at the head of the corps on the enemy's left. This desperate service was performed with the greatest determination and celerity at the charge, the corps led by Major Andrews, the Royal Scots by Lieutenant-Colonel McGregor Murray, without firing a shot, and they were well supported by their native comrades. Many fell from the destructive fire of grape, but the batteries and village were carried at the point of the bayonet.

The enemy's infantry fled, but the artillerymen stood to their guns, and all who were not bayonetted attempted to recommence a fire after the infantry had passed through them. The British and Mysore cavalry then made a brilliant charge on the enemy's right wing and completely routed it, and on the advance of the reserves under Sir Thomas Hyslop, the enemy's centre, which had not been attacked, finding their flanks turned, retired, but their artillerymen stood to their guns and served them to the last.

Orders were then sent to Sir John Malcolm to move on the enemy's camp, which he, however, found deserted. The flying enemy were pursued by the British cavalry and two light infantry battalions until nightfall.

After securing the enemy's camp the line returned to

the field of battle and there encamped, the sick and wounded and baggage joining it from the opposite side of the river.

The enemy lost about 3,000 men, with all their artillery (63 pieces of ordnance), together with their tumbrils, baggage, and camp.

The British losses comprised 778 men killed and wounded, including 38 European and 27 native officers ; most of the wounds were desperate, being chiefly caused by round shot and grape. A round shot struck amongst the band of the corps as they were marching towards the enemy, and knocked over five of the musicians.

The battle of Mahidpore was the last general action on a large scale fought in Southern India.   On the 2nd **1818** February 1818 the fort of Talnair on the River Taptee was stormed by the flank companies of the Royal Scots and of the Madras European Regiment ; the garrison was put to the sword, and the killadar, or commander, was hanged on a tree on the ramparts. Nearly 300 of the enemy were killed at Talnair, and of the British 25 men, including seven officers.

CHAPTER XXI

WHILST these operations were going on a force under Colonel McDowall, consisting of one company of foot artillery, two companies of Royal Scots, three companies of the Madras European Regiment, two sepoy regiments, five companies of Madras sappers and miners, a small battering train of the corps of sappers and miners, and some irregular horse, marched for the reduction of the Candeish hill forts.

1818

On the 2nd April the fort of Unkye was invested, but surrendered when summoned. Rajdier, on a high precipitous rock, was then invested. Colonel McDowall's summons was treated with contempt; consequently a battery of heavy guns opened on the 12th and kept up a heavy fire of shells, when towards evening the place caught fire and the garrison made its escape, but forty of them were brought in by the cavalry next morning and seven were found alive in the fort. Twelve guns were captured and some treasure dug out of the ruins. The fort of Inderye was evacuated the same night.

Many other forts were subsequently captured or surrendered, and on the 29th April the force set out for Chandoor, where it arrived on the 9th May, and on the 15th occupied Deharree, one march from Mallygaum.

The fort of Mallygaum was built of solid masonry with two lines of works, and was washed on three sides by the River Moose; the garrison was numerous and well provided. On the 28th May the attack commenced at daylight; the troops were exposed to a galling fire for some time, vainly attempting to enter the place. All the ammunition being expended, Colonel McDowall withdrew his camp and battering train to the pettah and sent for supplies; these arrived on the 9th June, when a heavy bombardment was opened. On the 12th the garrison offered to surrender on terms which were accepted, and Mallygaum surrendered on the 13th after a gallant defence. The British loss was 209 (including officers) killed and wounded, of which number the corps had twenty-five, including Major Andrews commanding the regiment, wounded.

During the siege of Mallygaum the detachment of the corps was particularly distinguished for its gallantry, and among the junior grades Serjeant William O'Brien and Corporal Thomas Tate, the latter wounded in the storm on the pettah, were very conspicuous. The fort of Ummulneir surrendered on the 25th November to a force under Colonel Huskisson, consisting of H.M. 67th Regiment, six companies of the Madras European Regiment, several sepoy regiments, the Madras sappers and miners, 250 irregular horse, and a battering train.

1819   In the beginning of the year 1819 the corps took part in the different combined movements into the Mahadeo Hills, and towards the end of February formed part of the besieging force marching against Asseerghur, a hill fort situated on the top of a precipitous rock 700 feet high, accessible in two places only, and these strongly fortified.

On the 17th March General Doveton took up his position before Asseerghur, his army consisting of the Hyderabad Subsidiary Force, partly composed of foot artillery, H.M. Royal Scots, H.M. 30th Foot, the Madras European Regiment, Madras sappers and miners, and two native regiments, and of Sir John Malcolm's division, and the Bombay brigade, composed of Bombay artillery, H.M. 67th Regiment, three native infantry regiments, and some pioneers.

Early on the morning of the 18th March the following party stormed the pettah : Five companies of the Royal Scots, the flankers of H.M. 30th, 67th, and of the Madras European Regiments, also five companies of sepoys and the Madras sappers, all under Lieutenant-Colonel Fraser of the Royal Scots.

The troops establishing themselves under cover in the streets of the pettah running parallel with the lower walls of the fortress, heavy batteries were formed and opened fire at 500 yards from the walls ; the enemy on the 18th made a sally which was repulsed, and a second sally made the same night was also repulsed, with the loss of Colonel Fraser killed, and several men killed and wounded.

On the night of the 31st March the breaching guns were placed in the new batteries and all opened fire with good effect.   The same day the Bengal division, under General Watson, C.B., arrived in camp, and by the 4th April the defences on each side of the entrenched breach were destroyed. On the 7th the breaching batteries again opened fire, made a practicable breach, and by 11 A.M. the next day the garrison accepted terms and all firing ceased.

Early on the morning of the 9th April the British flag was hoisted on the western tower of the upper fort under a royal salute from all the batteries ; at the same time the garrison, consisting of Muckranees, Arabs, and Scindees, descended into the pettah and grounded their arms.

The enemy's loss was trifling, as they fought behind walls, only 43 men being killed and 95 wounded.   The loss on the British side was 11 European and four native officers, 95 Europeans and 113 natives, rank and file, killed and wounded.   The corps lost 10 men and one officer, Lieutenant d'Esterre, wounded. The fall of Asseerghur closed the Mahratta campaign of 1817–18–19.

1824   In the beginning of the year 1824 the corps was upwards of 1,200 strong, and composed of a very fine body of men ; the flank companies were not surpassed by any, and equalled by but a very few regiments in the British Army.

On the declaration of war in Ava in 1824 the corps was one of those warned for the expedition to Rangoon. Out of 1,300 men composing it 863 of the most effective and healthy non-commissioned rank and file were picked for service; the remainder with two officers were left behind at Kamptee.

The regiment, under the command of Lieutenant-Colonel Hastings Kelly, with six captains, fifteen lieutenants, four ensigns, one surgeon, and three assistant-surgeons, embarked on board the transports *Bannerman, David Clarke,* and *George the Fourth,* and sailed from Masulipatam on the 13th April 1824. The rendezvous, Port Cornwallis in the Andamans, was reached on the 5th May, when the regiment joined the rest of the expedition.

Two days later the fleet sailed, entered the Rangoon river, and on the 11th May anchored off Rangoon. A slight fire was opened on H.M. ship *Liffy* from a battery on one of the wharfs, but it was soon silenced, when the troops landed and took possession of Rangoon, which they found abandoned.

The army was commanded by Sir Archibald Campbell, and the troops consisted of the Royal Scots, H.M. 13th, 38th, 41st, 44th, 45th, 47th, 54th, 87th, and 89th Regiments, together with the Madras European Regiment, the Governor-General's bodyguard, the 1st Madras Cavalry, the Madras sappers and miners, and twelve regiments of Madras native infantry, besides a powerful artillery.

On the 10th June a column, of which the corps formed

part, left Rangoon for the capture of the strongly stockaded fort of Kemmendine. Corporal Thomas Freer of the regiment was one of the first to volunteer for a ' forlorn hope' at a stockade about a mile from the fort, and was promoted to serjeant on the spot by the Commander-in-Chief. Colour-Serjeant O'Brien and Corporal Lucas were also particularly distinguished on this occasion.

After a heavy fire from our guns the regiment and other troops escaladed the stockade in spite of a determined resistance from the enemy, who lost 300 dead on the field, the regiment losing eleven killed and seventeen wounded ; the column then continued its march, and the following day reached Kemmendine, which was assaulted but found empty, the enemy having made their escape.

On the 6th August the fortified pagoda of Syriam was carried by a force of which the regiment formed part, the enemy making a very determined defence. On the 7th the regiment and detachments from other corps, under Colonel Kelly, assaulted the stockade of Dalla and carried it in gallant style, with the loss of fifty men killed and wounded.

On the 14th December Rangoon was set on fire ; the greater portion of the mess property and stores of the regiment was consumed on the occasion.

The stockade at Kokeen, under the Burmese General Bundoola with 25,000 men, was attacked on the 15th December by Sir Archibald Campbell, and carried after a desperate resistance. Corporal Thomas Tate of the regiment was promoted for his gallantry on this occasion. At this time sickness in the force was very great, and the regiment had lost 317 men, including those who had fallen in action or died of their wounds.

1825   On the 25th January 1825 part of the regiment proceeded with a force under General Calton towards Amerapoora, and on the 19th February attacked

K

and captured the Panlang stockades.   On the 7th March the immensely strong stockades of Donabew were stormed and carried ; Serjeant Gwyn of the Light Company was the first to enter.   Of the enemy, 230 were killed inside the stockade and 374 were taken prisoners.

1826   On the 1st January 1826 the stockade at Shoegheen was carried by a portion of the regiment, several men being killed and wounded. Sittang was also carried in January, and the assault was one of the sharpest and most brilliant actions that had taken place in Ava ; it was the last in which any part of the regiment was engaged, and ended the Burmese war, during which the regiment had on every occasion been conspicuous for its great gallantry.

On the 23rd July the regiment returned to Masuli-patam ; out of the 863 gallant men who had embarked from the same place in April 1824 about 100 only returned, and these broken down by privations and hard service ; nearly all the rest died in Burmah, more from disease and starvation than the sword of the enemy.

1827   On the 6th July 1827 news was received of the death of Sir Thomas Munro, Baronet, K.C.B., of the corps, Governor of Fort St. George, to whose memory an equestrian statue cast in bronze—by Chantry, and costing £8,000—was erected on the esplanade of Fort St. George, Madras.

In July also a very chaste and elegant silver-mounted snuff mull of the largest size was presented to the mess of the corps by Sir John Malcolm, K.C.B., K.L.S. The following inscription was engraved on it :—

' To the Madras European Regiment from Sir John Malcolm, K.C.B., K.L.S., in remembrance of Mahidpore.'

LIEUT.-COLONEL JAMES GEORGE SMITH-NEILL, C.B.

1830 On the 5th March 1830 the head quarters of the corps under Major Kyd marched from Kamptee towards Hyderabad (Deccan), a mutiny having broken out amongst the native troops quartered in that city. On the 26th April, when within sixty-three miles of the city, a dispatch was received at 3 P.M. ordering it to move on Hyderabad with the utmost expedition. The thermometer at the time in the coolest tents stood at 105 degrees. In less than two hours the ground was cleared ; the regiment (left wing) marched all night, rested during the excessive heat of the following day, continued its march most part of the night, and arrived under the walls of Hyderabad at seven o'clock in the morning of the following day without leaving behind a single man. Sixty-three miles including all stoppages in thirty-eight hours was a wonderful and almost unparalleled performance for Europeans in India during the hottest season of the year.

1833 In July 1833 intelligence was received in India of the death of Sir John Malcolm, G.C.B., of the corps on the 30th May.

This distinguished officer joined the regiment in 1781, and amongst the many illustrious men who have belonged to the Madras European Regiment, the name of Malcolm will ever be famous in Indian history. A statue to him by Chantry is erected in Westminster Abbey.

On the 14th July of this year, also, Sir Thomas Bowser, K.C.B., of the corps died in England ; he joined the regiment in 1773, was taken prisoner in Baillie's defeat, and continued a prisoner, heavily ironed, in the dungeons of Bangalore until 1784. He was twice Commander-in-Chief of the Madras army.

1840 On the 31st December 1840 new colours were presented to the corps at Kamptee by Major-General John Woulfe.

1841   In December 1841 new colours were again presented to the corps by Major-General Riddell. It is presumed that those presented in 1840 were accidentally lost or destroyed.

In bringing this record of the corps to a conclusion nearly two hundred years since its existence as a military body and almost one hundred after its formation into an adminis-trative battalion, it may without undue laudation be said that no regiment has done greater service to the State, none has ever surpassed it in gallantry in the field or good conduct in quarters, nor can any corps in referring to its past history more appropriately quote the motto—

'*Spectamur Agendo.*'

NOTE.—A continuation of the records of the 1st Battalion of the regiment from the year 1842 to 1905 has been most ably written and published by Colonel Godfrey Bird, D.S.O., lately commanding the 1st Battalion The Royal Dublin Fusiliers.

APPENDICES

I

IN March 1841 the following highly complimentary order was received at regimental head quarters, and was subsequently published to the Army in the General Orders by Government of the 21st March 1841.

Immediately after its receipt it was read to the regiment, paraded for that purpose.

'The Right Honble. the Governor in Council, having had under consideration the many honourable services of the 1st Madras European Regiment, whose career is to be traced through the most eventful periods of British India, has been pleased to order, that in commemoration of its victories under Lawrence, Clive, Sir Eyre Coote, Lord Cornwallis, and other distinguished generals, it shall bear, emblazoned on its colours, the motto " Spectamur Agendo," and the names of the following battles, and expeditions, in which it has borne part:—

' " Arcot," which it successfully defended under Lord Clive in 1751.

' " Plassey," to which place it accompanied Lord Clive in 1756, and assisted in the victory gained on 23rd June 1757.

' " Condore," where it greatly distinguished itself under Colonel Forde, in December 1758.

' " Wandewash," for the victory on the 20th January 1760.

' " Sholinghur," where it fought with success, on the 27th September 1781.

' " Nundy-Droog," which it assisted to capture in 1791, and for which his Lordship in Council is pleased to permit it, also, to bear a " Royal Tiger " on the colours and appointments.

' " Amboyna "—" Ternate "—" Banda," to which islands the regiment proceeded with the expeditions in 1796, and 1809-10.

' " Pondicherry," the corps having been employed at the sieges, and reduction, in 1761-78 and 1793.

' In reviewing the services of this gallant regiment, the Right Honble. the Governor in Council has had before him various records of its employment in the early wars in the Carnatic, and in Southern India, of which the present brief notice gives but a general indication, and for which it is but necessary to refer to the military operations at different times, near Trichinopoly, from the year 1746 to 1761, to its share in the resistance against the French, under Lally, Conflans, Bussy, Law, and other enterprising commanders ; its various engagements in the Northern Circars, and Cuttack, and its service in Ceylon in 1795–96.

'The 1st European Regiment was actively employed throughout the campaigns against Hyder Ali and Tippoo ; during the latter, it assisted in the storming of Bangalore, and in the engagement near the walls of Seringapatam, under the command of Lord Cornwallis, and already does it bear on its colours testimonials of the last Mahratta war, in which it was present at the sieges of Talnair, Malligaum, and Asseerghur, and of the bravery and devotedness which were so conspicuous in Burmah.

'The Right Honble. the Governor in Council feels that in conferring these distinctions upon the 1st Madras European Regiment, he does but accord a tribute of well-merited honour to the army of Fort St. George, and his Lordship is assured that the decorated banners of its oldest corps, whilst exhibiting a proud memorial of past achievements, will never cease to wave over soldiers, whose good conduct in garrison, and bravery in the field, will well maintain what has been so nobly won by their predecessors in arms.'

Extract from General Orders by Major-General Riddell, commanding Hyderabad division :

'Secunderabad, February 12, 1842.

.   .   .   .

'The distinctions lately conferred on the 1st Madras European Regiment have shown the character of that corps when employed in the field, and it will now be the Major-General's gratifying duty to represent in its merited colours their steady discipline in garrison. *Nothing* could exceed the good conduct, temper, and firmness exercised by the men, when brought into contact with the natives. No fault in any individual tended in the slightest degree to detract from the *perfect discipline* evinced by the corps ; thus proving that all felt that the character of the British soldier is to be upheld, not alone by bravery in action, but steadiness and orderly conduct in quarters ; and Major-General Riddell feels assured that this fine corps will ever continue to deserve the high opinion now entertained of it.'

II

Various Organisations of the Regiment

1766 Up to 1766 the corps always consisted of three battalions. In 1766 the corps was formed into three regiments, each of nine companies.

1774 In 1774 the three regiments were reduced to two, of two battalions each.

1784 In 1784 the four battalions were formed into four distinct regiments, of one battalion each.

1796 On the 8th January 1796 the four regiments were reduced to two regiments.

1830 In January 1830 the two regiments were formed into one, the 1st Regiment forming the right wing, and the 2nd the left wing.

1839 On the 16th August 1839 another regiment was raised, and named the 2nd Madras European Light Infantry, when the old corps was again designated the 1st Madras European Regiment.

1843 On the 11th April 1843 the designation of 'Fusiliers' was conferred on the regiment, and they were known as the 1st Madras Fusiliers.

1853 In 1853 a third regiment was raised, and known as the 3rd Madras European Regiment.

1862 On the incorporation of the East India Company's European troops with those of Her Majesty Queen Victoria in 1862, Her Majesty was pleased to confer on the regiment the title of 'Royal,' and from the 30th July it bore the name of the 102nd Royal Madras Fusiliers.

1881 In 1881 the regiment became the 1st Battalion The Royal Dublin Fusiliers.

NOTE.—The 2nd Madras European Light Infantry is now the 2nd Battalion of the Yorkshire Light Infantry.

The 3rd Madras European Regiment is now the 2nd Battalion of the Royal Inniskilling Fusiliers.

III

Roll of Commanding Officers of the Corps

1748 Major Stringer Lawrence.
1756 Robert Clive.
1758 John Caillaud.
1766 Joseph Smith.
1768 John Wood.

1769 Ross Lang.
1778 John Braithwaite.
1782 Eccles Nixon.
1784 Sir Henry Cosby, Bart.
1785 Robert Kelly.

1785 Charles Frazer.
1785 Robert Chesshyre.
1785 Thomas Bridges.
1785 Robert Gibbings.
1786 George Smith.
1786 Francis Ward.
1786 Edward Collins.
1786 James Edington.
1788 Matthew Horne.
1788 Thomas Bruce.
1795 George Cunningham.
1795 Richard Tolson.
1795 Thomas Trent.
1795 Joseph Bicliff.
1797 Sir Thomas Bowser.
1804 John Long.
1806 James Innes.
1807 Aldwell Taylor.
1809 Sir John Malcolm.
1817 Augustus Andrews.
1819 James Kelly.
1823 Hastings M. Kelly.
1827 Gilbert Waugh.
1829 John Lindsay.
1830 Hugh Kyd.
1832 Charles A. Elderton.

1838 James Kerr.
1840 James A. Howden.
1841 James Wahab, C.B.
1841 James Bell.
1843 Robert J. Vivian.
1844 Charles Butler.
1846 Thomas A. Duke.
1852 William Hill, K.C.B.
1854 East Apthorpe, K.S.F.
1856 Daniel H. Stevenson.
1857 James G. Smith Neill, K.C.B.
1857 Michael Galwey, K.C.B.
1859 Thomas Fisher.
1861 Richard Shubrick.
1862 Thomas Raikes, C.B.
1870 John Blick Spurgin, K.C.B.
1872 Henry J. Jepson.
1876 George John Harcourt.
1879 John Duncan.
1884 William Cleland.
1887 William F. Vetch, C.V.O.
1890 Charles R. Kerr.
1894 William C. Riddell.
1898 George A. Mills, C.B.
1902 Spencer Godfrey Bird, D.S.O.
1906 Archibald John Chapman.

IV

ON the regiment leaving Nagpore in 1840, a very handsome marble tablet was put up in the church at Kamptee, on which was the following inscription :—

' Sacred

To the memory of the undermentioned officers and men of the 1st Madras European Regiment, who died at or near Kamptee during the time the troops served in the Nagpore Subsidiary Force.'

[Here follow the names and dates of death of five captains, four lieutenants, and five ensigns of the regiment, and also of nineteen serjeants, two drummers, fourteen corporals, and 390 privates, whose remains are interred in the churchyard adjoining.]

' *This Tablet*

Is erected by the officers of the 1st Madras European Regiment on the occasion of the corps quitting the station in the year 1840, as a token of their esteem and regard for their deceased brother officers and soldiers.'

V

On the 5th November 1799 the Governor in Council published the following list of officers permanently posted to the corps :—

' EUROPEAN INFANTRY

The Madras European Regiment—Colonel J. BRAITHWAITE, M.G.

Lieutenant-Colonels.

G. Fotheringham.
James Oram.

Majors.

A. Beatson.
P. C. Desse.

Captains.

1. T. G. Gray.
2. William Sheppard.
3. W. Davidson.
4. And. Maccaley.
5. Adam Ormsby.
6. D. M. Holford.
7. C. D. Bruce.

Captain-Lieutenant.

John Brown.

Lieutenants.

1. John Butler.
2. Thomas Steel.
3. Matthew Stuart.
4. Broughton Dodd.
5. Thomas Vaughan.

Lieutenants—cont.

6. John Fortune.
7. George Pippard.
8. Thomas Ogilvie.
9. G. J. Forbes.
10. G. Lang, Junior.
11. H. R. Barker.
12. P. B. Man.
13. Francis James.
14. Gilbert Briggs.
15. James Moore.
16. L. W. Hall.
17. J. Turner.
18. T. H. Smith.
19. T. C. Gordon.
20. Gilbert Waugh.
21. C. Stewart.
22. M. Bt. Kinsey.

Adjutant.

Francis James.

Quartermaster.

J. Fortune.'

At this time the uniform of the regiment was as follows :—

A uniform jacket, with light-blue facings and gold embroidery ; black leather stocks, with false linen collar one-third of an inch deep ; white linen waistcoats, single-breasted and cut round, with metal regimental buttons, the same as those on the jacket ; white nankeen pantaloons, with half-boots, and black round hats, ornamented in such manner as the officers commanding the regiment thought proper.

Swords according to the present pattern to be worn, with a buff shoulder belt. The breastplate to be of whatever pattern the commanding officer might deem proper.

The officers of the European Regiment, when off duty, were permitted to wear uniform coats, with the same facings, epaulettes, and embroidery as directed for the uniform jacket.

VI

THE following is a copy of the inscription on the monument in the church at Dunchideock, erected by Sir Robert Palk, of Haldon near Exeter, to the memory of Major-General Stringer Lawrence in 1775 :—

> ' For Discipline Established,
> Fortresses Protected,
> Settlements Extended,
> French and Indian Armies Defeated,
> Peace Established in the Carnatic.'

(The above was taken from the monument in Westminster Abbey.) Then, underneath a trophy of colours, drums, arms, &c. :—

> ' Major-General Stringer Lawrence, who
> Commanded in India from 1747 to 1767.
> Died 10th January 1775, aged 78.

> The desperate state of affairs in India
> Becoming prosperous by a series of victories
> Endeared him to his country.
> History has recorded his fame.
> The regrets of the worthy bear testimony to his virtues.

> Cui Pudor et Justiciæ soror
> Incorrupta Fides Nudaque Veritas
> Quando ullum invenient Parem.

> Born to command, to conquer and to spare,
> As mercy mild, yet terrible as war,
>   Here LAWRENCE rests.
> The trump of honest fame from Thames to Ganges has
>   proclaimed his name.
> In vain this frail memorial Friendship rears :
> His Dearest monument are Armies' tears.
> His Deeds on fairer columns stand engraved
> In Provinces preserved and Cities saved.
>   A. MORE.'

There stands also, in the park at Haldon, on the highest point in the woods, called Penn Hill, a very large tower erected in honour of General Stringer Lawrence. The tower is triangular, with smaller towers at the corners. It contains three rooms on its three floors. In the centre of the ground floor room is a statue of the General in a Roman toga. The tower stands 1,000 feet above sea level, and is a landmark for 100 miles round.

This tower was erected by Sir Robert Palk, Baronet, sometime Governor of Madras, in 1788, an eye-witness of the triumphs in war and of the virtues in peace of his illustrious friend.

The following inscriptions are written on the three walls, on large tablets of black marble with gold lettering :—

South Tablet.

' To the memory of Major-General Stringer Lawrence, who for the space of twenty years commanded the British armies in India, and by his superior genius, consummate skill, and unremitted exertion, with an inferior force extinguished the power of France, restored the glory of the British name, and by replacing in the Government Mahomed Aly Cawn Bahadur, the distinguished son of Anaverdee, in happier times the rightful sovereign of the Carnatic, established the empire of Britain in Hindustan.

' Nor were his talents in war more eminent than his milder virtues. He aspired to and attained a name more glorious than that of conqueror. He was the deliverer of India. At his approach every village poured forth its inhabitants. Every eye was riveted with attention on his person, and he seemed, while blessings in different languages and from every side were showered upon him, to have blended in one family (of which he was the common father) the natives of Europe and the inhabitants of Asia.'

West Tablet.

'The Princes of India revered him as a superior being, and to the end of his life their testimonies of affection were unceasing. The following inscription (from the original Persian), sent after his death, perpetuates the gratitude of the Nabob of Arcot—" To the memory of the late Major-General Stringer Lawrence, His Highness the Nabob Wallajah, Ameer Aly, Hind Separ Sahlar, Prince of the Carnatic and the ally of His Britannic Majesty, has caused this inscription to be placed in testimony of his friendship, and of the high sense he entertains of the important services rendered by the General to himself and to his friends the English in India."

' As he was the first founder of the English power in Hindustan, the opinion entertained by the East India Company of his merits and services is best expressed in the monument which at the public expense they caused to be erected to his memory in the Abbey Church of Westminster.'

North Tablet.

'This excellent man was born at Hereford in the year 1697. His early days were devoted to that service of which in the following years he was so bright an ornament. He served against the rebels in 1745 as aide-de-camp to Lord Tyrawly, and at Gibraltar he was long the much-loved patron of General Wolfe. At the solicitation of the East India Company he accepted the command of their forces in the Carnatic, and after having saved and extended the provinces he closed his long career of military glory by his successful defence of Madras, the capital of the British possessions, in the year 1759. He died full of years, fuller of honours, in 1775, and his remains are deposited within sight of this Tower, in the parish church of Dunchideock.'

GLOSSARY

Caffir (negro soldier).

Choultry (native rest-house).

Killadar (commander of a fortress).

Lascar (a native employed with guns or tents).

Nawab (a Mussulman prince).

Peon (a messenger; also the designation of the first native troops employed).

Pettah (the native town outside a fortress).

Rajah (a Hindoo prince).

Sepoy (a native soldier).

Soobah (the viceroy of a province).

Tondiman (the chief of the Poligars).

Topass (a half-breed soldier, so called from his being employed as interpreter).

INDEX

L

MAP OF
SOUTHERN INDIA

Statute Miles
0   20   40   60   80

FIELD-MARSHAL H.R.H.
ARTHUR WILLIAM PATRICK ALBERT, DUKE OF CONNAUGHT AND STRATHEARN,
K.G., K.T., K.P., G.C.B., etc.
Colonel-in-Chief The Royal Dublin Fusiliers.

www.ingramcontent.com/pod-product-compliance
Lightning Source LLC
Chambersburg PA
CBHW030403100426
42812CB00028B/2820/J